FIRE
at Will

Terminating Your Employees Legally

From the editors of
The HR Specialist

CONTRIBUTING ADVISER
Anniken Davenport, Esq.

EDITOR
Kathy A. Shipp

EDITORIAL DIRECTOR
Patrick DiDomenico

ASSOCIATE PUBLISHER
Adam Goldstein

PUBLISHER
Phillip A. Ash

ISBN 1-880024-03-9

This publication is designed to provide accurate and authoritative information regarding the subject matter covered. It is sold with the understanding that the publisher is not engaged in rendering legal or financial service.

CONTENTS

INTRODUCTION

Employers like to think they can run their business as they see fit, hire the best people, fire the deadwood and build a profitable operation. After all, that's the American dream, right?

As is often the case, reality doesn't match the dream. New interpretations of long-standing laws can snare unsuspecting employers. Many bosses are learning that recent regulatory moves and court decisions limit their autonomy in the workplace. Axing unproductive workers can trigger expensive litigation. Even as the economy slowly recovers, employers encounter obstacles at every turn.

Employees have rights, and employers who even unwittingly violate them face years of legal repercussions. Even if they ultimately prevail in court, employers will have spent thousands in legal fees. As the old adage goes, an ounce of prevention is worth a pound of cure.

The good news is that employers have rights, too. There are legal ways to terminate unproductive and dishonest employees.

Fire at Will provides you with information on the most recent laws, regulations and court decisions to keep your business operating legally. You can stop waste, ensure worker safety and keep drugs out of your workplace by aligning your manuals, policies and practices with the guidance in this special report.

If you don't know the law, all the hard work you have put into building your business can be washed away in a tide of litigation. *Fire at Will* shows you how to protect your business from frivolous, baseless lawsuits by training your managers and supervisors to comply with key employment laws, and do it while enforcing effective workplace policies.

In *Fire at Will* you'll learn how to make employment laws work for you, not for the workers you terminated.

— 1 —

YOUR ULTIMATE RIGHT (AND MOST POWERFUL WEAPON)

*P*ete MacNamara stood overlooking the work floor of his bindery. His father had started the business in a garage after the Depression and built it into a profitable corporation and secure place of employment for his workers. Pete had taken over the top slot 10 years ago, when his dad died. Today, what Pete saw nearly broke his heart.

One man was sitting on a pallet truck, reading a book. Two women who were supposed to be operating gluing machines were spending more time chatting than working, while unfinished books were piling up. Off in a corner, a kid from the mail room and a forklift operator had just walked through an emergency exit that was supposed to be locked. Pete figured that they were either doing drugs behind the building or stealing from the company.

It was a typical day in the shipping department. In fact, Pete reflected, it was a typical day in the whole operation. Either the workers couldn't see him, or they just didn't give a damn that he was up there. They knew he couldn't fire them. Pete felt like selling the business. It was such a disgrace to the memory of his dad, who never would have stood for the behavior Pete was witnessing without firing someone or everyone. But, Pete reflected, times had changed. His hands were tied by miles of legal red tape.

YOUR RIGHT TO FIRE

What's MacNamara's problem? He, like other owners, feels powerless to make firing decisions that would have seemed like foregone conclusions only a generation ago. Since he doesn't understand how to get rid of unproductive workers, he does nothing.

Sure, a proliferating jungle of federal, state and local laws protects workers, and you need to be on top of them and exercise caution to avoid running afoul of them.

But none of the laws can deprive you of your right to fire substandard employees—provided you exercise your ultimate power as an employer without discrimination and back it up with appropriate procedures that protect you from legal action.

Remember: It's your right to fire underperforming workers. In fact, there are virtually no workers you can't discharge, provided you carefully document their performance, show that your grievances against them are justified and don't base your decision on any illegal, discriminatory motive. If you've been tolerating poor performers for a long time, you may not be able to fire them tomorrow. But rest assured: By following the procedures outlined in this special report, you can discharge them soon.

Chances are you know which workers aren't pulling their weight: those who are chronically absent or unproductive without good reason or whose behavior puts others at risk. So what's stopping you from handing out pink slips? Most likely, you haven't been keeping extensive, fully documented records so that you can establish just cause for any eventual terminations. We urge you to start keeping such records today.

Write it down whenever you or a supervisor issues a warning, disciplines an employee or suggests how to improve performance. Don't rely on the worker's supervisor to back you up later if the discharged worker decides to make a fuss. Obtain a report in writing from the supervisor today—before he or she leaves the company or retires. *Remember:* A lawsuit can come your way long after a termination.

Above all, don't forget the Golden Rule of employee management: Objective documentation is your single most effective weapon in any type of legal action. This means having an accurate, up-to-date job description for each position and establishing objective performance measures for each of the job's essential functions.

TYPES OF DOCUMENTATION

The types of documentation you should keep in employees' files:

- Job application.
- Performance evaluations.
- Time and salary records.
- Documentation of any verbal or written warnings or suspensions.
- Documentation of employees' knowledge of company policies and work rules (e.g., a signed acknowledgment form from the employee handbook).

Title VII of the Civil Rights Act of 1964 requires employers to maintain records for one year from the date the record was made or the personnel action was taken, whichever is later, on actions such as layoffs, transfers and demotions. (Other federal laws, such as the Age Discrimination in Employment Act, and state laws may require you to keep such records for a longer or shorter period.) The Department of Labor (DOL) requires employers to maintain most wage records for at least three years.

Nowadays, employers must maintain work-related emails as well as any paper documents in the event they may be needed in a court proceeding. In fact, the moment an employer knows of a potential lawsuit, it should identify and preserve all paper and electronic communication related to the litigation. The EEOC advises employers to preserve all pertinent communication "until final disposition or action."

AT-WILL EMPLOYMENT

Assert your right to fire at will by requiring all employees to sign an at-will statement specifying that you may terminate them at any time for any reason or *no* reason. Similarly, employees may leave for any reason or no reason. The statement, which can be part of the employee handbook, also should clearly stress the employee handbook isn't a contract of employment.

Your right to fire isn't absolute. You may not fire employees for an unlawful reason: i.e., because of their age, race, sex, disability status, religion, skin color or their refusal to obey an unlawful order. Make sure you have a legitimate reason for the firing and fully document it.

Of course, if your workers are covered by a collective bargaining agreement, you must follow the procedures set forth in it.

MAKING YOUR COMPANY 'SUE-PROOF'

If a fired employee can prove that even an *implied* contractual relationship existed between employer and employee, any resultant legal cases may be much harder—and more expensive—for you to win. But this risk can be eliminated almost completely if you take appropriate action and integrate the following practices into your organization's policy:

➤ **Review all employee literature.** This includes recruitment ads and brochures, company handbooks and manuals (including confidential ones), policy statements and other official literature for language that could imply a contractual relationship. Eliminate all references to "permanent" employment, and change any references to "discharge for good cause" to "discharge at management's discretion." Your employee handbook should have numerous disclaimers stating that the handbook is not a contract. Place a disclaimer in each handbook section because employees often do not read it from cover to cover. Also, update the handbook at least annually and have the employee sign that they have received the handbook and understand that it is not a contract.

➤ **Instruct those involved in recruiting not to oversell the company.** Give written instructions to interviewers on what statements to avoid (such as "Your only limit is your own ability" or "You have job security just so long as you perform well"). Reiterate this policy every time you provide training.

➤ **Consider inserting an at-will employment statement in employment applications.** This is a statement to be signed by applicants indicating that their possible employment with the firm is strictly "at will," and that any changes in such policy can be effected only by a written agreement signed by a designated representative of the organization.

➤ **Consider limiting the authority to make employment offers to only a few managers.** Their offers should be in writing and should contain at-will provisos and this caveat: The offer supersedes any oral promises that the interviewer may have made. Even when you make your position clear on your right to fire, such statements are not litigation-proof. You can still be sued for illegal discharge, but the statement tends to discourage such suits and puts your position upfront.

The at-will doctrine has been interpreted differently by courts in various states. Some state courts presume that a handbook creates a binding contract while others make the opposite assumption. These decisions have hinged on the actual wording of the handbooks themselves. Remember, the law interprets any contract ambiguity against the party who wrote the contract. That means the employee always gets the benefit of the doubt.

—2—
How to Fire a Worker Without Fear of Being Sued

Marjorie MacLean felt great about the way her department was shaping up. Since moving up from the ranks to supervisor, she had hired three people and got rid of some deadwood. Team spirit was running high. The day before, the company president had commended her on how well things were going.

So when he called her into his office, she was astonished to see him looking ashen and shaken. He told her that one of the workers she had fired—a chronic underperformer—had filed suit against the company. The worker claimed that he had been a victim of age discrimination because one of the people she had hired was younger than he was.

As Marjorie walked down the hall to start assembling documents as to why she had let the man go (and she hoped that her predecessor's records were good enough to protect her), she felt her elation evaporate. Why did this have to happen now?

Wrongful-Discharge Suits on the Rise

Technically, you may terminate at-will employees at any time for any reason. But if a discharged employee can prove you fired him for an illegal reason, prepare to write a large check to him as well as to your attorney.

The perfect storm for employment litigation is bearing down on employers. Laws passed in response to corporate corruption, war and an aging, more diverse workforce have swelled the number of employees under federal protection. Additionally, an activist National Labor Relations Board has expanded the employee protections that the National Labor Relations Act provides.

For example, employees who report illegal activity they have witnessed on the job have numerous protections at both the federal and state levels. The Occupational Safety and Health Administration has become a one-stop shop for whistleblower protection, administering 22 different federal whistleblower laws. Fire an employee who has whistleblower protection and prepare to fight federal and/or state enforcement officials.

Additionally, the nation's expanded military commitments have drawn reservists from the workforce. Those in the Reserves and the National Guard have legal rights to reinstatement on their return from duty. The Uniformed Services Employment and

Reemployment Rights Act (USERRA) effectively prevents employers from terminating workers because of their military obligation.

At the same time, we have an aging workforce. Baby boomers are delaying retirement or starting second careers and constitute a growing segment of the workforce The Age Discrimination in Employment Act protects workers age 40 and older. Also, since they're more likely to be disabled, employers may have to accommodate them under the Americans with Disabilities Act.

Americans' increasing longevity has created another issue for employers: Employees are more likely now to take time off under the Family and Medical Leave Act to care for their elderly parents. And, since 2009, the FMLA allows employees to take military family leave to care for family members who suffer a serious injury or illness while on active duty or to address issues related to military deployment.

Factor in employees who claim they've been fired because they filed a workers' compensation claim or had a legitimate reason for absenteeism, and it may appear that everyone's protected by some federal law, and firing is impossible. It's not.

➤ **Observation:** Increasingly, former employees are filing defamation suits claiming that their reputations were damaged when managers told other workers the reason for their firing. For example, in one case a worker claimed that an executive defamed him by announcing he'd been fired for taking part in a conspiracy to misappropriate company funds. The court ruled that because the announcement was made in a closed-door meeting of executives, it was a privileged communication to people with a "legitimate and direct interest" in the information. The fact that word spread around the company afterward was beside the point, the court said.

In contrast, you should be careful how you inform rank-and-file workers about an employee's dismissal. Some lawyers advise that you not bring up the subject.

When employees ask, be discreet; avoid making a direct accusation. You're better off legally if the fired worker talks instead of you.

AVOIDING IMPLIED CONTRACTS

Even if a worker has not signed an employment contract with your company, a court might find that an *implied* contractual relationship exists. Depending on state law, a court may conclude that an implied contract exists if employee handbooks, policy manuals and oral statements directly or indirectly allude to job security.

Examples:

- **An employee manual** stated that during the probationary period employees could be terminated without notice. Thereafter, they became "permanent."

- **A supervisory manual** stated that the company's policy was to terminate employees for "just cause" only.

- **An interviewer asserted** that the applicant would stay with the company "as long as he did his job."

The lesson? Go over your employee manuals now! Don't have one? Then it's time to get cracking. Also, make sure that those who are interviewing and hiring applicants know what types of statements to avoid when discussing an applicant's future with the company.

Some courts have also found implied contractual relationships in cases where an employee had made a special sacrifice in taking the job, or the employer had significantly benefited from his or her contributions. Other courts have held that the totality of the parties' relationship must be reviewed to determine if the employer's conduct gave rise to an implied promise that it would not act arbitrarily in terminations.

One legal authority writes that by far the most troubling incursion on the at-will doctrine is the "covenant of good faith and fair dealing." This means that regardless of what you say or do to make it clear to certain employees that you can fire them, the law will prevent you from exercising that discretion unless you do so fairly and in good faith. Although that's probably how you want to treat your employees, a jury may second-guess your view of what is fair or in good faith.

➤ **Recommendation:** Although not all states recognize the covenant of good faith and fair dealing, it's a good employment practice for you to follow.

ARBITRATION AGREEMENTS

Some employers are implementing arbitration agreements as a way to cut down on litigation, but the agreements are not a panacea. The agreements generally require employees to take any dispute to arbitration rather than court as a condition of employment. By keeping the dispute out of federal court and in front of a neutral arbitrator, cases can be decided quickly and inexpensively without setting a precedent. Arbitration agreements help employers avoid the bad publicity a trial can bring.

The U.S. Supreme Court has handed down two key arbitration decisions. In *Circuit City v. Adams*, 532 U.S. 105 (2001), the court ruled that mandatory employment arbitration agreements generally are enforceable. Even though employers won the right to use arbitration agreements, subsequent decisions have severely limited their effectiveness. When the Circuit City case went back to the 9th Circuit Court of Appeals, it acknowledged the employer's right to require arbitration, but found that this particular agreement was so one-sided that it wasn't enforceable under state law. (*Circuit City v. Adams*, 279 F.3d 889, 9th Cir., 2002)

In its second decision on arbitration agreements, the Supreme Court ruled that the agreements aren't binding on government agencies that enforce the law. An employee had sued Waffle House under the ADA even though he'd signed an arbitration agreement. At the same time, he filed a complaint with the EEOC. The restaurant maintained he must settle the matter through arbitration. But the EEOC pursued the case anyway, noting that it hadn't signed any agreement. The court sided with the EEOC. (*EEOC v. Waffle House*, 534 U.S. 279, 2002) Your arbitration agreement can keep your employee out of court, but not the feds.

The National Labor Relations Board ruled that if "reasonable employees would construe the [arbitration agreement's] language to prohibit" protected activity under the National Labor Relations Act, then the arbitration agreement isn't lawful.

Caution: Don't try writing "home-made" arbitration agreements. They should be crafted by skilled attorneys who are up to date on all recent decisions. Talk to your attorney to see if arbitration is right for your organization.

What You Don't Have to Tolerate From Unions

*W*hen Gerry Haynes pulled into the parking lot at his printing plant, he immediately noticed a large blue Lincoln that didn't belong to any of his workers. Two men stood behind it, and he recognized them as union organizers—the same men who had visited his plant several times in the past to try to organize his workers. He saw that several of his workers had stopped to collect printed materials from the men, while others hurried by without stopping to talk.

Gerry had no problem with the organizers being there, and he knew that his workers were free to talk to anyone they wanted. He had always felt secure in the past, and for good reason. He prided himself on being a good employer—someone his workers could really count on to stand by them.

But would that still be enough this time? Faced with a flat business cycle and cash flow problems, Gerry had been forced to make some layoffs last year. He felt reasonably sure that his workers would still stand by him. But this time he was not as confident as he had been the last time the two men stood in his parking lot handing out fliers.

NATIONAL LABOR RELATIONS ACT

Despite your best efforts, a dissatisfied employee makes contact with a union and becomes a potential Trojan horse for the union inside your company. Your first response is likely to be one of outrage, a feeling of betrayal. Although you have many defensive rights in meeting a union campaign, acting against that employee isn't one of them.

Discrimination against employees who initiate a union campaign is prohibited by Section 8(a)(3) of the National Labor Relations Act (NLRA). Employers who discharge an employee, discriminate with regard to tenure or any term or condition of employment and are found in violation can be required to reinstate the employee with back pay. Should the union effort result in a representation election and you, the employer, win, that victory could be set aside and you could be ordered to bargain with the defeated union.

If you own or manage a smaller firm, you could be one of a series of targets in the same region or industry that the union has decided to stake out. This makes for greater efficiency and bigger returns for the union. You have every right to contact other employers that may also be in the union's sights and to share strategy.

UNIONS TODAY: A PROFILE

After decades of decline, union membership has bottomed out below 12% in recent years. Several factors have been fueling a pro-union backlash: the unions' "Change to Win" initiatives, the perceived excesses of Wall Street and high-profile employment law violations by mega employers such as Wal-Mart. Unions have also sponsored the push for a higher minimum wage, known as the "Fight for 15." As a result, unions are organizing more National Labor Relations Board (NLRB) elections. Over the last several years, unions have won about two-thirds of workplace elections.

In 2015, the National Labor Relations Board approved what some called a "quickie election rule" that shortened the time between when a union election was approved and when voting took place. Many business groups called the rule the "ambush" election rule, but the early returns do not show a significant boost for unions. The rule took effect in April 2015 and resulted in 150 more elections in 2015 than 2014, but unions continued to win at the same rate.

The NLRB's *Browning-Ferris, Inc.* decision in 2015 could potentially make it easier for unions to organize. The Board adopted an expanded definition of joint employer for organizing purposes. As a result, unions are now targeting franchises and contingent employers in their unionizing efforts.

YOUR RIGHTS IN A UNION-ORGANIZING CAMPAIGN

Labor law gives your rank-and-file employees the right to join a union. Assuming you prefer to operate as a nonunion company, what are your rights? You have the right to express your views in an effort to persuade your employees not to join a union, and you also have the right to run your business.

The U.S. Supreme Court dealt employers a victory in 2008 in *Chamber of Commerce of the United States et al. v. Brown*. The ruling overturned a California law

---

MORE INFORMATION ABOUT UNIONS

The appearance of a union could be a sudden surprise. You might have no information on its background or where it's been active. Where do you find what you need? Your local and state industrial and trade associations, as well as the economic development councils responsible for bringing industry into your area.

In a broader context, a key source of information on union-organizing efforts is the monthly National Labor Relations Board's *Election Report*, which summarizes details of union campaigns. For more information, go to **www.nlrb.gov**.

that restricted some employers' rights to communicate with workers during union drives. The case underscores the fact that you have the right under the NLRA to communicate your views with employees during a union-organizing campaign. Use and protect these rights by exercising caution and controlling your own behavior. Here are some tips:

➤ **Don't act emotionally or with a feeling of betrayal.** Be sure you have a thorough knowledge of the labor law rules and seek expert help. Conventional wisdom won't suffice, nor will your own determination of what's fair, no matter how objective you think you are.

➤ **Present your side and get the hearing you want** by following the game plan that the law allows. It may appear too restrictive, but you clearly have weapons available. Despite labor law pitfalls and restrictions and the frustrations they may cause, you can emerge intact from a union's organizing campaign.

Whatever route you choose—whether to accept the union or resist it—you can exercise your rights effectively. Make sure you do so systematically, lawfully and intelligently. Also, remember: Just because a union-organizing campaign is under way doesn't mean you have to relax worker discipline. You can hand out punishment for infractions of rules even to the most vocal of the union sympathizers as long as you can show that the sanctions are consistent with the way you handled similar situations before the organizing drive began.

What makes a company an attractive target? Employee dissatisfaction, mostly. Unions will pick up complaints from disgruntled employees about any number of the following:

- Job insecurity.
- Inadequate compensation and benefits.
- Perception of inequitable treatment.
- Impersonal attitude of the supervisors.

- Lack of standards or feedback.
- Lack of opportunity.
- Poor communication, from senior management on down.

NLRB FLIP-FLOPS ON *WEINGARTEN* RIGHTS

Good news: Employees in nonunion workplaces no longer can insist that co-workers be present during investigatory meetings. You can legally deny such employee representation requests thanks to an NLRB ruling, which was the board's fourth flip-flop on this issue.

Background: In 2000, the NLRB greatly expanded employee rights by ruling that even nonunion employees were allowed to bring co-workers to investigatory meetings or interviews if the employees believed the meeting might lead to disciplinary action. But in 2004, the board reversed itself, saying that nonunion employees *don't* have such *Weingarten* rights, which are named after the 1975 court case that established the rule. Employees at unionized businesses still retain their *Weingarten* right to representation.

What you <u>can't</u> do

The National Labor Relations Board applies strict rules of conduct to an employer during a union's organizing drive. Make sure that you don't:

✓ Discriminate in *any* way against any employee for participating in union activities. This prohibition applies to all aspects of employee relations, including decisions regarding tenure and the terms and conditions of employment.

✓ Promise or grant benefits to your employees (such as wage increases, holidays, benefits or improved working conditions) to encourage them to abandon the union.

✓ Make threats based on employee support of the union, including threats of discharge, layoffs, plant closure or discontinuing current benefits.

✓ Interrogate your employees or prospective applicants concerning union organizing activities.

✓ Prevent pro-union oral solicitation by employees during *nonworking hours* and *breaks*, or prohibit union insignia on shirts and jackets.

✓ Bar workers from wearing logos on their clothing. The NLRB has determined that broad bans on logos could deter workers from wearing pro-union messages.

✓ Engage in surveillance of employees to determine their positions regarding the union, or photograph employees engaged in protected activity.

✓ Take a straw vote of employees as to whether they favor or oppose the union, except in special circumstances and in accordance with legally mandated procedures designed to protect employees. (Consult your legal counsel.)

✓ Refuse to hire or consider for hire a union individual even if you know that the person's only purpose in seeking employment is to organize your employees.

✓ Adopt work rules that restrict discussion about compensation and benefits.

✓ Dominate or interfere with the formation or administration of any labor organization or contribute financial or other support to it.

Although not necessarily unfair labor practices, the following conduct may result in the invalidation of an election:

✓ Campaigning on *company time* and *premises* within 24 hours of an NLRB-scheduled election. Meetings held off-premises may be conducted under special circumstances.

✓ Reproducing and distributing official NLRB ballots and showing employees how to mark them.

✓ Discussing the union with employees in a supervisor's office, regardless of the non-coercive tenor of your remarks.

✓ Prohibiting distribution of union literature in nonwork areas during nonwork time, such as in the lunchroom during the lunch hour.

✓ Requiring employees to wear "Vote No" buttons in the plant.

What you can do

You may hold meetings with your employees on company time and property to answer questions and discuss the company's position on unionization. Just make sure the meetings aren't held in a supervisor's office. Talk with employees at their own workstations or in a group meeting.

You can mail literature to the employees' homes, stating the company's position, but be careful what you say. Some other things you can do:

✓ Prohibit a nonemployee from entering private property unless that individual or union has no other reasonable means of access to customers or employees.

✓ Describe the good features of working for your company, such as existing benefits, job security and steady work.

✓ Remind employees that signing union authorization cards does not mean they must vote for the union.

✓ Inform them of the disadvantages of belonging to a union, such as the possibility of strikes, serving on picket lines, paying dues, fines and assessments. Point out the sky-high salaries that union officials receive.

✓ Explain the meaning of the phrases "dues checkoff" and "union shop."

✓ Inform them about any prior experience you have had with unions and what you know about the particular union that's trying to organize them. Remind them that unions are a business, and the organizer is a sales rep.

✓ Tell your employees how their wages and benefits compare with other unionized and nonunionized companies with less desirable packages.

✓ Correct any unproved or misleading statements made by union organizers.

✓ Disclose the names of undesirable persons who may be or have been active in the union, provided this is accurate information verified by official sources. **Caution:** Your claims must be true or you could be sued for defamation.

✓ Inform them that, insofar as their status with the company is concerned, they are free to join or not to join any organization.

✓ Express the hope that your employees vote against this or any union.

A lawfully waged campaign may defeat an organizing drive. Violation of the rules of conduct, however, can result in invalidation of a company-won election or certification of a union that lost an election. It is important, therefore, that you seek legal advice promptly.

➤ **Observation:** You don't have to bend over backward to cooperate with unions either. In a recent court of appeals decision, a company had refused to let union organizers post notices of their upcoming meetings on a company bulletin board. The NLRB ruled this discriminatory because the company had allowed other kinds of worker notices to be posted. But the appeals judges said that the only notices previously allowed on the bulletin board advertised things such as puppies or used cars for sale. Those are not the same as using the board for meeting notices, the ruling said, so it was not discriminatory to say "no" to union backers.

WHY AN EMPLOYEE SHOULD *NOT* WANT A UNION

Union membership is costly. In addition to monthly dues (averaging $20–$50), there can be periodic assessments ("voluntary") to such union organizations as COPE (Committee on Political Education). Dollars to COPE may go to support candidates with views diametrically opposed to a member's. After the initial campaign all new employees required to join the union are also obligated to pay an initiation fee, which can range from $50 to $200 in some unions. Also:

■ **Through strike assessments,** employees may be obligated to give financial support to striking workers at other companies.

■ **The union is an equalizer.** Under the union concept every employee is the same. Only length of service (seniority) is important—not ability or merit.

■ **The only real weapon the union has is to strike.** When that occurs, employees lose wages, which are usually never recovered, and employers are compelled to physically exhaust the supervisory staff and take other extraordinary measures to continue providing services to clients.

■ **Employees who participate in an "economic" strike** can be permanently replaced by their employer.

■ **Local union members often have little say** concerning their own employment. Usually, orders have come from the national or local office of the union.

■ **A union's primary interest is not in an employee** as an individual but rather as a source of income and power. Unions can, and sometimes do, bring with them strikes, bad feelings and even violence on occasion.

Caution: If you try to pick and choose the meetings you think are worth publicizing and those that aren't, you will have a hard time showing a judge that you weren't discriminating against union supporters. Also, you must not seem to be designing a policy for bulletin boards, email or other communications channels that appears to target unions. Put a policy in place—and strictly adhere to it—when there's no threat of unionization in the air, and it will stand you in good stead should the organizers later target your company.

With regard to email use, beware. In one case, an administrative law judge at the NLRB ordered Prudential Insurance to hold a new union election because the company distributed anti-union emails but didn't allow organizers to access the system. The NLRB ruled that the company held an unfair advantage. So, whatever medium you use to campaign against unions, allow employee organizers to use it for pro-union messages.

DEALING WITH UNION ENCROACHMENT

Let's say you become a unionized employer: that the union has won the representation election. Suddenly, after running your own business, you've got a partner. No more unilateral decisions in dealing with your employees.

The key question: How do you protect yourself in your decision-making and thus prevent union encroachment on your prerogatives as a boss, including your right to terminate deadwood employees? It may seem ironic, but your best defense is something that comes with a union: the negotiated contract. The contract language spells out your management rights. So what you do in negotiating that contract (the goals you formulate) is vital to protecting your interests.

Through the years, decisions of the NLRB and the courts have tended to narrow management's rights, in what has seemed to be an invasion of business decisions. An example is the area of subcontracting, interpreted to involve "terms and conditions of employment"—the definition for union involvement. Even such issues as dropping a product line, automating or moving a plant and having an in-plant cafeteria or food vending machines have been held to be subject to bargaining.

In negotiating a contract, nail down your right to make a wide variety of business decisions. The contract language becomes your protection because it will surely be scrutinized if a dispute with the union arises.

You'll want to assert your rights in a variety of contract clauses, such as the right to discipline for absenteeism and the right to discharge for excessive time spent away from work. Arbitration clauses (another factor that can seriously intrude on your rights) should meticulously define which issues in conflict are to be dealt with exclusively by an arbitrator. At the same time, avoid going overboard with a blanket management-rights demand aimed at covering all bases. In its decisions, the NLRB has interpreted this strategy as an effort to strip the union of its statutory prerogatives by holding that it was not a good-faith approach to bargaining.

Be aware of other pitfalls to avoid. In case the contract language is imprecise where your rights are concerned, you should have an accurate record of contract negotiations to fall back on. This means keeping a well-documented account of bargaining history—throughout all contract negotiations. In addition, the practices you follow with the ongoing contract can affect your rights. If you relax discipline or give benefits not called for, these concessions can become an inherent part of the company relationship with the union, without benefit of contract language.

In all these areas you'll want the benefit of legal counsel. Your own rule of thumb in the process should be to retain your rights to the maximum extent possible. Remember: The union will assign a negotiator with years of experience. Make sure your representative is equally skilled and understands what's at stake: your right to run your business. The first round of negotiations is the most important. Rights that you give away now will be hard to win back later.

4

YOUR RIGHT TO
TEST EMPLOYEES FOR DRUGS

*O*ne day at lunchtime, Jack Davis made a change in his usual routine. A large crowd was waiting for the elevator, so he decided to take the stairs to the ground floor of the building. As he opened the door to the stairwell, he heard a few words spoken one floor below him, followed by hurried shuffling and the sound of a door slamming. He thought little of it until he reached that floor, where an acrid smell choked him and made his eyes water. "Drugs," he thought. "Thank heavens, it probably wasn't someone on my staff."

But then he thought again and realized that if drug users were anywhere in the company, they wouldn't respect departmental boundaries. And he began to wonder what he should do to monitor and protect his staff.

YOUR BEST DEFENSE: PREVENTION

When drugs don't seem to present a problem within a company, it's easy to develop a cavalier attitude about them. That's not very smart. Drug abuse often begins with a single offender and then spreads out malignantly. You've heard that productivity takes a nose dive and the company's overall health may be threatened. What you may not realize are the horrible effects drugs may be having on some of your most valued employees, some of whom you even may consider your friends.

Experts say your best defense is to detect drug abuse when it first appears and get your employees the help they need as soon as possible. That's easier said than done. But always remember that people are your business. Without them, you aren't in business at all. By staying in touch, you'll know what is normal behavior for them and be able to notice when something is off-center. Signs to look for include:

- **Accident proneness.** Some drugs interfere with eye-hand coordination, causing employees to stumble or fumble with equipment.

- **Inattention or forgetfulness.** Sometimes a supervisor's request or instructions may fail to register with an employee who's a little high.

- **Absenteeism.** Be suspicious of increased use of sick days. Drug users miss work about twice as often as other employees. Also look for patterns: Calling in sick on days before or after long weekends may signal a substance abuse problem.

- **Personality change.** Cocaine and crystal methamphetamine ("meth") users will experience euphoria when high. Cocaine users later will often become irritable or depressed while meth users can become violent.

- **Insomnia or twitching.** Heavy "meth" users sometimes reach a stage called tweaking, when they are awake for days at a time. They may experience uncontrolled twitching during this period.

- **Sudden increase in productivity.** In the early stages of cocaine use, some individuals perform better because the drug accelerates their heart rate, increases blood pressure and stimulates their nervous system. Opioid abusers can show bursts of energy that then give way to fatigue.

- **Falling productivity.** Marijuana makes some people inattentive to deadlines or unable to gauge quality. Over time, cocaine interferes with the heart and nervous system, causing mental and physical dysfunction. Opioid use ultimately leads to lowered productivity, fatigue and depression.

- **A chronic runny nose.** Snorted cocaine irritates the mucous membranes.

If you have noticed signs of possible drug abuse, take these steps:

React to performance problems. If an employee suddenly becomes clumsy around a dangerous machine, reassign him. If output has slipped, counsel the individual to improve. Focus on performance, not on your suspicions about the cause.

Ask the employee to tell you what he or she thinks is wrong. But make no accusation about drug use. Doing so may violate the Americans with Disabilities Act.

DEVELOP A DRUG ABUSE POLICY

You have to know your goals because drug abuse policies vary depending on the particular nature of the work site. Some points to consider:

■ **The policy should be clearly written,** posted, frequently communicated and uniformly enforced regardless of rank or position. It should set rules on the use and abuse of drugs, control procedures and disciplinary action to be taken.

■ **If you have a pre-employment drug detection test,** issue fair warning on your job application forms. Also, an employment agreement should clearly state that drug testing will be a routine part of a person's employment.

■ **Be consistent—drug-test everyone.** Failure to drug-test all applicants or similarly situated employees could result in discrimination charges.

■ **Employee handbooks should be reviewed regularly** for consistency with other company policies and compliance with existing federal, state and local regulations.

■ **You should add a statement** in the handbook asserting that management may revise its drug policy at its discretion.

■ **Current illegal drug use isn't a disability** under the ADA, but *former* and *recovering* users are protected under the act *(see Section 11)*.

The U.S. Department of Labor has a tool designed to help employers develop their own drug-free workplace policy. It is available at **http://webapps.dol.gov/ elaws/drugfree.htm.** The Partnership for a Drug-Free America also provides good information on its website: **www.drugfree.org.**

SETTING UP A DRUG TESTING PROGRAM

Be sure your drug testing program passes legal muster. States often specify the labs and testing procedures you can use and the manner in which you must keep test records. It's not necessary to set up the program on site. You may prefer to use out-side local laboratories that handle these tests. Make a special point to ask labs about their quality-control procedures. What documentation do they keep in handling specimens to prevent any mix-up? How long do they keep such records? How well do they document the chain of custody for each specimen? The answers to these questions may prove vital if test results ever end up in court.

Legal issues for the employer: Based on court and arbitration rulings, companies appear to be safe in administering drug tests in these situations:

1. During pre-employment, provided your state law doesn't prohibit this.
2. During a fitness-for-duty test of an employee who has job performance problems.
3. After the occurrence of a preventable accident.
4. When there's a reasonable suspicion of substance abuse.

Where labor unions are involved, many drug testing issues will be addressed in the collective bargaining agreement.

Currently, 48 states and the District of Columbia have statutes regulating employee drug testing, and some allow it only in very limited circumstances or in a narrow range of job categories. (A handful of cities and counties as well have their own drug testing laws.) Be sure to check with an attorney familiar with your state law before implementing any drug-testing program. Also, check the Department of Transportation's regulations for any drug testing required of commercial drivers.

Blood and urine analyses are the most common types of drug tests used, but they are not foolproof. To prevent lawsuits, follow the manufacturer's testing and sampling instructions, and advise employees of what to expect if a test is found positive for drug use.

Note: Special rules apply to public employers, who are subject to the dictates of the Fourth Amendment, which outlaws unreasonable searches and seizures. Because drug testing can be considered an unreasonable search under this amendment, public employers should consult further with their attorneys on requirements for drug testing.

TREAD CAUTIOUSLY

When you have to fire someone, be sure you have follow-up or confirmatory tests on file, with bulletproof documentation. You should not base your action on the result of only one unconfirmed positive test. Failure to confirm tests properly can subject employers to employee lawsuits on various common-law grounds: defamation, wrongful discharge, intentional infliction of emotional distress or negligence.

Supervisors and managers should never discuss the results of a drug screening with anyone other than those who have a need to know. If an employee is terminated because of a positive test or refusal to submit to testing, others should merely be informed that the employee violated company rules.

➤ **Observation:** You can't force applicants or employees to submit to drug tests, but you can refuse to hire the former or discipline the latter if they refuse to be tested. Be aware, though, that a wrongful-discharge claim can be used to challenge the termination of an employee who refuses to be drug tested or who tests positive. Consult with your attorney before terminating someone under those circumstances.

Avoid intrusive monitoring, such as the use of closed-circuit cameras that monitor "private" places like restrooms and changing rooms, because some state courts tend to be liberal in their interpretation of invasion of privacy. In most states individuals have the right to be protected against unwarranted intrusions into their private lives and can enforce such rights under the tort of invasion of privacy, also known as intrusion upon seclusion. In determining whether an intrusion is highly offensive to a reasonable person, courts look not only to when the drug test is done but also the manner in which it's conducted. Close monitoring of employees as they give urine samples, for example, might be more suspect under the intrusion-upon-seclusion test.

Although invasion of privacy is the primary concern for employers, you should also check your state law because some states incorporate the prohibition on unreasonable search and seizure from the Fourth Amendment. In addition, some states make it a crime to observe employees in places where they have a reasonable expectation of privacy, such as a restroom stall. You should also check with counsel before recording audio in the workplace. Audio recording violates some state wiretap laws.

While state laws vary, random drug testing is the most likely form of testing to be struck down as an invasion of employee privacy. Random testing may be permitted in situations where there's a reasonable suspicion of drug use or the job involves public safety or the safety of others.

Reasonable-suspicion drug testing is usually permitted. However, defining "reasonable suspicion" has been difficult and involves consideration of these factors: the nature of the information regarding the drug use; the reliability of the informant; and the degree of corroboration and other factors contributing to the suspicion. Some states have specifically defined "reasonable suspicion." Consult with your attorney for additional information.

Note: The Drug-Free Workplace Act of 1988 requires all organizations receiving procurement contract awards of $100,000 or more and all recipients of federal grants to provide a drug-free environment for their employees. It requires you to discipline, fire or require drug abuse rehabilitation for any employee convicted under any criminal drug statute as a result of a workplace drug violation. Covered employers must also disseminate a substance abuse policy and inform employees of the company's policy and the consequences of violating it. (The law does not extend to subcontractors or subgrantees.)

➤ **Recommendation:** The Center for Substance Abuse Prevention conducts research on the effects of drugs on job performance. Its research chemists can provide technical advice on setting up drug testing programs. They can also refer you to outside attorneys who are well versed in the legal aspects of drug testing. For additional information, go to **www.workplace.samhsa.gov**.

5

How to Combat and Cure Chronic Absenteeism

*M*ary DeFrancisco was furious with Paul Marcus, one of the customer service phone reps she supervised. He had called in sick again, forcing the other employees to pick up the slack. Paul was averaging one sick day every two weeks. It simply wasn't fair. "Please get Paul on the phone for me," Mary said to one of her staff.

As she sat angrily at her desk, she thought about how she would let Paul have it for showing so little respect for his colleagues. But then she had a sudden doubt. What, legally, could she say to Paul? Would the fact that she had called him at all mean that she was harassing him? Suppose she fired Paul, and he sued for harassment? Would she be fired—and all because she was trying to manage as effectively as she knew how?

PROACTIVE STEPS

Nothing's more infuriating than a chronically absent worker. Many employers get caught up in a cycle of repeated attempts to reform these types. That's a mistake because the costs of employee absenteeism—reflected in lost production, overtime and temporary replacements for the absent worker—can add up quickly. In fact, some personnel experts estimate that an absent employee costs a company 1.75 to 2.5 times his or her daily salary. Some large companies estimate that absenteeism may be costing them more than $500,000 per year.

How can employers combat the problem? Approaches vary, but most successful absenteeism programs include three elements: a clearly enunciated company policy, careful documentation and consistent application of the policy.

Have a clear policy

Frequently, absenteeism problems arise because a company has no clear policy. A company policy statement should be distributed to all employees, indicating when and under what conditions an employee will be paid (or not paid) for absences. Determinations can be based on average absence rates for a company or industry based on a survey of what other companies offer. The policy should clearly state which absences are excused and which are not.

The policy should indicate types and stages of discipline that will apply to employees who violate the policy, as well as *positive measures* and awards that will accrue for individuals or departments that meet zero-absence targets.

Caution: No-fault policies, which allow employees to accrue a set number of absences within a specified time period regardless of the reason, can lull employers into a false sense of security. Employers must know which absences count as leave under the Family and Medical Leave Act and be able to note time off used as an accommodation under the Americans With Disabilities Act. Any tracking system that doesn't note these types of absences leaves an employer flying blind into a lawsuit.

Always document absences

Documentation is a cardinal rule in any activity for which an employee may be disciplined. You should keep attendance/absence records for all employees. An *absence rate* can be figured by dividing the number of days an employee was scheduled to work for a given period into the number of absences. You can also calculate average absence rates for each department and for the company as a whole.

Be consistent

No company policy is going to remain effective unless it is applied consistently and fairly to all employees.

For this reason, supervisory personnel should be clear on their responsibilities for recording data and for counseling and disciplining employees. Yet, an absenteeism policy must also remain flexible enough to allow for special problems and situations that might arise. (Lack of flexibility is one of the reasons most often given by professional arbitrators for overruling company disciplinary actions arising from employee absenteeism.)

Perhaps the most important point you can make concerning absenteeism is that a sick leave or absence policy isn't a benefit to be equated with vacation time or personal leave. The more employees understand this and recognize your commitment to disciplining chronic absenteeism, the fewer problems you're likely to have.

USE POSITIVE DISCIPLINE

When you're faced with an employee who is chronically absent, it's best to have a positive discipline program in effect. For example, assume that a worker has an absenteeism problem resulting in lower productivity. Because absenteeism typically comes under the "minor problem" category, the first step is a precounseling session between the individual and his supervisor. In this session the supervisor determines if the employee understands the company's policy on absences. The positive discipline approach then consists of the following stages:

■ **Oral reminder stage.** This stage follows the counseling session and lasts three months or however long seems to be in the company's best interest. But the period has to be uniform for all employees. If you resolve the problem, the slate is wiped clean and so is the documentation of the incident.

(Continued on page 22)

SUPERVISORS' GUIDE TO CUTTING ABSENTEEISM

Say your company has an absenteeism policy in place, but you're still experiencing a high rate of absenteeism. It may be a good idea to sit down with your managers and supervisors and plan a strategy.

Here's what others have done in similar situations:

Provide outlets for dissent. Not all absenteeism is capricious. When people are denied outlets for their job pressures, they tend to run from them. If you make dissent possible by encouraging people to speak up, hearing them out and, where feasible, acting on what you hear, they realize they don't have to escape from the workplace to let off steam.

Cut the drag of boring work. You can't eliminate tedious work. But you can try to reduce a person's need to flee from it. Here are two suggestions:

- Expand boring jobs so that employees can see their tasks through to a worthwhile result. Giving work a beginning, a middle and an end increases at least threefold the satisfaction to be gained from it.

- Break down boring jobs into smaller pieces so that a variety of tasks can be distributed among more people.

Use incentives. Extra pay for showing up is not a radical idea, and it's relatively cheap. The concept of "well pay" instead of sick pay has proved itself and can be easily adopted. For example, for each authorized (paid) sick day people do *not* use by year's end, they get paid for a day and a half. Or let employees bank sick time to be used against a future disability. These kinds of arrangements can be a magnet to the workplace.

Try gimmicks. They're only good for the short term, but they're also reusable from time to time. Try a departmental contest: For example, the person with the lowest number of absences in a three-month period wins an oversized turkey. Use gimmicks sparingly, but play them up when you do. (Just be sure to include those who were absent for FMLA reasons.)

Explain how absenteeism affects everyone. When people feel easily replaceable, they think they won't be missed. If you tell them why they're needed, they won't want to stay away. Each employee is in some way a specialist; taking the time to point this out makes each one feel skilled, valued and needed.

Provide worthwhile training. Employees who are continually learning new skills stay engaged, motivated and have lower absentee rates. Also, if you cross-train employees when appropriate, you will gain more scheduling flexibility.

HOW TO ASSESS THE IMPACT OF ABSENTEEISM

A few specific questions will help you take a realistic measure of losses:

✓ Has work remained undone because people were out?

✓ Have department work schedules been disrupted?

✓ Have completion deadlines or shipping schedules been missed because absentees slowed down the work?

✓ Has your personal work schedule been knocked awry because you had to juggle assignments? Find replacements? Do on-the-spot training for fill-in employees?

✓ Have departmental costs risen because absenteeism has led to work being spoiled by replacements failing to perform as well as the regulars? Lower productivity? Overtime work?

(Continued from page 20)

■ **Written reminder stage.** If the problem still exists after the counseling session, a second session between the employee and the supervisor is scheduled. This time, however, the supervisor writes a memo spelling out the problem, the worker's acknowledgment of it and his or her agreement to work toward its resolution.

A copy is placed in the employee's personnel file. The written reminder stage lasts six months, or however long you think is best for the company. If the problem is resolved within this time, the memo is considered inactive and there are no repercussions for the worker. However, keep the memo in the employee's file.

■ **Decision-making stage.** If the absenteeism problem still exists after the written reminder stage, the supervisor has a final meeting with the employee and spells out the company's policies again. Then the employee is given a one-day leave of absence to decide whether to continue working for the company on condition that he or she agrees to abide by its rules.

An issue related to absenteeism is whether you can legally terminate an employee who routinely has to take time off because of service obligations to the Reserve or National Guard. The Uniformed Services Employment and Reemployment Rights Act (USERRA) gives workers have an absolute right to the time off because of their service obligations—even if it is inconvenient for you—and a job has to be waiting for them when they return. But it doesn't have to be the same job, just one with the same status, pay and benefits as the previous one. So be sure that you can objectively show that the new job is of equal status.

Caution: In addition to USERRA, employees may take leave for service related activities related to deployment or to care for a next of kin with a service related medical condition under the FMLA. Employers may not discipline employees for absences protected by the FMLA and ADA. *(See Sections 6 and 11.)*

Another related issue is whether an employee's excessive absenteeism is the result of a serious health condition. If so, or if you're not sure, be aware that you may have legal obligations under the FMLA or the ADA. *(See Sections 6 and 11.)*

——— 6 ———

YOU DON'T ALWAYS HAVE TO OK FAMILY LEAVE

*B*ob Markowitz realized that his firm, which provides management services to commercial buildings, would falter without Norma Garrett's efficient way of keeping records straight and putting out fires with customers. He told her so openly and frequently.

When she was away for even a week's vacation, turmoil ensued. Other staff members who were briefed to fill in for Norma just didn't measure up.

That's why Norma's news came as such a blow: Her mother was facing a regimen of chemotherapy, and Norma felt she must go to Florida to be with her for two months. Bob couldn't think of anyone on his staff who could adequately fill in, and he doubted that anyone from a temp agency could grasp the ins and outs of the business. He also figured that no one would want to put the energy into learning the intricacies of a job that would last only a couple of months.

THE FMLA'S IMPACT

When the Family and Medical Leave Act (FMLA) took effect in 1993, it dramatically changed the way an employer can deal with a worker who has a serious health condition, a new baby, or a sick spouse or parent. But the law has limits as well, so its impact on your operations may not be as devastating as you think.

Start with the basic requirements. The law provides eligible employees up to 12 weeks off for the birth or adoption of a child, the employee's own serious health condition or to care for an immediate family member with a serious health condition.

The law also provides for two types of military leave: military exigency leave and military caregiver leave.

FMLA leave is an entitlement, and employers may only deny it in limited circumstances. For example, married couples working for the same company are limited to a total of 12 weeks of leave between them to care for a newborn or a newly adopted child. Similarly, employers can warn key employees that they are not entitled to return to their job if doing so would cause the employer grievous economic harm.

The law only covers employers with 50 or more workers. That includes a company in which the payroll numbered 50 or more for any 20 weeks in the current year or the preceding year. All employees within a 75-mile radius are lumped together to determine if this limit is met. That means a manufacturer with 40 employees at the plant site and 15 more at a distribution center in a town 30 miles away is covered.

But a business with 45 employees working at its headquarters in Massachusetts and five each working in sales offices in Chicago, Atlanta and Los Angeles is exempt from the law's requirements even though it has more than 50 on the payroll.

Caution: Some states have enacted family leave legislation covering employers with 50 or more employees regardless of location, while other states require smaller companies to provide leave. If your company is near the 50-employee limit, there are ways you can keep the firm out of the law's reach. Are new hires, who will put you over the threshold, really needed as employees, or could independent contractors accomplish the same tasks?

Similarly, if you're considering two sites for a secondary location and one is inside the 75-mile radius and one outside, the opportunity to avoid the FMLA's requirements might be a reason for choosing the more distant site.

WHO'S COVERED?

To be eligible for FMLA leave, an employee must have worked for the same employer for at least 12 months (not necessarily consecutively) and clocked at least 1,250 hours during the 12 months before taking leave.

When feasible, you may want to hire more part-timers to prevent the disruption associated with long family leaves. As with a decision to use independent contractors rather than employees, you wouldn't want to opt for part-timers solely to solve the potential family leave problem. Still, it is an important consideration to throw into the balance when you are weighing alternatives.

The law has a loophole allowing an employer to refuse to hold open jobs of key employees: those among the highest-paid 10%. Although you must grant them leave and continue their medical benefits, the company is not obligated to guarantee that an appropriate job will be waiting for them when their leave is over. But for each person denied that promise, the company has to show that filling the job on a full-time basis "is necessary to prevent substantial and grievous economic injury to the employer's operations."

To show that you couldn't keep the job open until the employee's return, it probably won't be enough to point out how important it is. You'll have to show why your efforts to deal with the tasks on a temporary basis were unsuccessful, perhaps including records of attempts to persuade a retiree to return for the interim or to find adequate talent through professional temp services.

An employer must grant FMLA leave to eligible employees for their own serious health condition, that of a sick child, spouse or parent or to care for a new child in the family (by birth, adoption or caring for a foster child).

Note: The DOL has advised employers to use a broad interpretation of the definition of "son or daughter" under the FMLA. It clarified that any employee who assumes the role of caring for a child will receive parental rights under the FMLA, regardless of the biological or custodial relationship.

For example, an employee who cares for a domestic partner's child—or whose partner gives birth or adopts a child—is now eligible to take FMLA leave to care for the child. That means it also covers FMLA leave for extended family members: For instance, an uncle who is caring for his sick niece while the child's single parent is called into military duty is eligible for leave.

Since the Supreme Court ruled that Section 3 of the Defense of Marriage Act was unconstitutional, the FMLA provides the same benefits to same-sex couples as it does to opposite-sex couples.

FMLA regulations also permit employees to take up to 26 weeks of unpaid FMLA leave in each 12-month period to care for family members who have suffered a serious injury or illness while on active military duty. To be eligible for this type of leave, the service member must have designated the employee as "next-of-kin." Also, families of all active duty military personnel are allowed to take up to 12 weeks of job-protected leave per year to manage their affairs under certain qualifying circumstances.

EMPLOYER RIGHTS UNDER THE FMLA

You don't have to take an employee's word about a medical condition that may qualify for FMLA leave. You have the right to demand medical certification from the employee's health care provider.

To qualify, the employee's condition must meet the FMLA's definition of a "serious health condition." The law says a serious condition must involve more than three consecutive calendar days of incapacity plus "two visits to a health care provider." Those two visits must occur within 30 days of the period of incapacity, as clarified in the revised FMLA regulations.

DOL regulations allow you to directly contact an employee's health care provider to seek clarification about information on an employee's FMLA certification form. *Note:* An employee's "direct supervisor" is prohibited from making such inquiries. The rules give this right only to a "health care provider, an HR professional, a leave administrator (including third-party administrators) or a management official." Also, employers can't ask doctors for information beyond what is required by the certification form.

Keep in mind that unpaid family leave is meant to be a last resort for employees who have no other way of coping with an emergency. That means you can insist that all vacation time and personal leave days be used up concurrently with FMLA leave and all allotted sick leave, in cases when the leave is for a personal illness.

Courts have made it clear, however, that an employer must keep FMLA leave days exempt from the company's no-fault absentee policy.

Employers should develop a consistent leave policy that provides rules for all types of unpaid leave, including USERRA, ADA and FMLA-covered absences. The policy should clearly state how paid leave, vacation and sick leave days are to be used when an employee takes FMLA leave.

LEAVE TIME

Eligible employees can take up to 12 weeks of unpaid FMLA leave during a 12-month period. Under DOL regulations, you must set a fixed 12-month period for all employees based on one of these measuring-year methods:

- A calendar year.
- A "leave year," such as your fiscal year.

- A year mandated by state law.

- A year starting on the anniversary of the employee's date of employment.

- A rolling period, starting on the date the employee first took FMLA leave.

The last scenario above is the most difficult to administer, but it would prevent an employee from "stacking" 24 weeks of leave at once: that is, 12 weeks at the end of one year followed by 12 weeks at the beginning of the next year.

Be careful to select a tracking system. FMLA regulations state that employees can choose the method that benefits them the most if the employer has failed to elect a method.

In states with more generous leave provisions than the federal law—a number allow workers to take as many as 16 weeks—the state statutes apply.

If the reason for the leave is the birth of a child, you can insist that the employee take the time off in one lump sum and then return as soon as possible, provided that the employee isn't adversely affected: that is, when the leave time provided isn't sufficient to cover the actual period in which the worker is needed at home. But if the reason is a chronic serious health condition—the employee's own illness or that of a child, spouse or parent—the worker has the right to take the time off intermittently. That means, for example, sharing the care of a sick parent with siblings by taking two weeks off each month. Or an employee can request a work schedule that lets him or her take the leave in half-days, working mornings only.

Remember that the 12-week total is cumulative. An employee who already has taken four weeks of leave can come back later the same year and demand eight weeks for another emergency.

You can insist on 30 days' notice when the cause of the leave is predictable—say, pregnancy or elective surgery. You can also insist that the leave be scheduled to minimize inconvenience, when the employee has options.

AFTER FMLA LEAVE

The law requires employees to keep you informed of their changing situations, how treatment is progressing and when they expect to return to their jobs.

If the 12-week period has expired and the employee can't return to work because he's still ill or caring for a relative, the employer's FMLA obligation ends. (In some circumstances, however, you may have to grant leave under the Americans with Disabilities Act as a reasonable accommodation if the employee has a qualified disability. Check with your legal counsel on whether any potential ADA liability exists.)

If the employee decides not to come back for any other reason—she's found a better job or wants to spend more time with her new baby—you can demand repayment of all costs incurred to maintain her health insurance while she was on leave.

What's likely to be your biggest headache? Having the proper spot for the returning worker. You have several options. Using a temporary worker to fill in during the leave allows the worker to seamlessly return. Cross-training workers in a department can minimize the impact of any absence by allowing co-workers to step in and then step out when the regular worker is ready to return. Remember, the employee is not entitled to the same job back, merely an equivalent one in terms of pay, benefits, responsibility and prestige.

Caution: Unlike many federal anti-discrimination claims, the FMLA allows for individual liability on the part of supervisors. That means your personal assets are at risk if the employee wins an FMLA lawsuit.

CHECKING FOR ABUSE

It's difficult to determine if an employee may be abusing your FMLA policy. To safeguard compliance, be sure that all documentation supplied is complete and satisfies any questions you may have regarding the medical condition. Generally, employers may request recertification every 30 days, but if the employer suspects abuse and can document those suspicions, it can seek certification more frequently.

Employers should also ask healthcare providers for an anticipated return to work date. Employers may request recertification if the employee asks for leave beyond that date.

One of the hardest tasks for employers is keeping track of "intermittent" leave: when an employee takes off a few hours, a single day or a week as determined by his or her needs. Thus an employee can use FMLA time to take certain days off spread over many months for chemotherapy, for example, or some other medical treatment that qualifies under the law. Those who would rather work a four-day week can potentially abuse this benefit by spacing the days off at one per week for 60 weeks before exhausting their allotted leave time of 12 weeks (or 480 total hours). Because the 12-week limit for FMLA leave begins again every year, a worker might restart benefits from scratch by using them up intermittently.

Employers who consistently ask for certification as frequently as the law allows minimize abuse. Also, employers who disagree with the initial certification can pay for a second opinion. If the two opinions disagree, the employer may pay for a third opinion and all parties must abide by the third opinion.

STATE LAWS

Several state legislatures are debating proposals to add new mandates to their state family and medical leave laws, including expanded parental leave and leave rights for domestic violence victims. Twelve states already require leave for employees to attend children's school activities or other forms of parental leave. California, New Jersey and Rhode Island require paid FMLA leave, funded by a payroll tax on employees. San Francisco recently added paid leave for employees, partly funded by employers and partly by the California payroll tax system. New York state has also added a paid leave provision, funded by a payroll tax. In addition, an Executive Order has established paid sick leave for employees working under federal contracts.

─7─

DON'T DISCRIMINATE
AGAINST PREGNANT WORKERS

*M*ark Dawson took pride in running a family-oriented business and placed a high priority on worker satisfaction. But as more of his female employees reached their prime childbearing years, his policy of granting paid maternity leave and then unpaid leaves of absence was beginning to cause operational problems. He could not afford to hire additional staff to help during times when he was understaffed.

Should he change his previous policies? Could doing so land him in legal trouble? He realized that it would be unfair to change his policies regarding the next request for maternity leave, after the others had enjoyed more liberal treatment.

He was committed to providing a great working environment, but he also realized that it would not be possible for long if he allowed profits to slump and then had to make layoffs.

PREGNANCY DISCRIMINATION ACT

Not many years ago, pregnant women were subject to poor treatment from employers and company insurance plans as well. But the Pregnancy Discrimination Act (PDA), enacted in 1978, prohibits discrimination on the basis of "pregnancy, childbirth and related medical conditions." The PDA forced most employers to make wholesale changes in their maternity leave, disability pay and health insurance policies.

The law requires all employers to treat disabilities caused by pregnancy and related conditions the same as other temporary disabilities under any health, disability, insurance or sick leave plan including workers compensation. It also prohibits discrimination based on a woman's ability to become pregnant, such as policies that exclude women of childbearing age from certain jobs.

A woman also cannot be denied a job or promotion merely because she is pregnant or had an abortion. She cannot be fired because of her condition, nor can she be forced to go on leave as long as she is physically capable of working. Women who take maternity leave must be reinstated under the same conditions as employees who return from leave following other temporary disabilities.

The EEOC has published a series of questions and answers that clear up most of the law's ambiguities. Some court decisions have provided answers as well.

1. What workplace actions are prohibited under the PDA?

An employer cannot fire, refuse to hire, demote or take any other adverse action against a woman if pregnancy, childbirth or a related medical condition was a motivating factor in the adverse employment action. The PDA prohibits discrimination with respect to all aspects of employment, including pay, job assignments, promotions, layoffs, training and fringe benefits (such as leave and health insurance).

An employer is required under the PDA to treat an employee temporarily unable to perform the functions of her job because of her pregnancy or a related medical condition in the same manner as it treats other employees similar in their ability or inability to work, whether by providing modified tasks, alternative assignments or fringe benefits such as disability leave.

2. Does the PDA protect individuals who are not currently pregnant based on their ability or intention to become pregnant?

Yes. The PDA's protection extends to differential treatment based on an employee's fertility or childbearing capacity. Thus sex-specific policies restricting women from certain jobs based on childbearing capacity, such as those banning fertile women from jobs with exposure to harmful chemicals, are generally prohibited. An employer's concern about risks to a pregnant employee or her fetus will rarely, if ever, justify such restrictions. Sex-specific job restrictions can only be justified if the employer can show that lack of childbearing capacity is a bona fide occupational qualification (BFOQ); that is, reasonably necessary to the normal operation of the business. *(See also Question 7.)*

An employer is also prohibited from discriminating against an employee because she has stated that she intends to become pregnant. Thus, demoting an employee with a good performance record two weeks after she informed her manager that she was trying to become pregnant would constitute evidence of pregnancy discrimination.

3. May an employer ask an employee or applicant whether she is pregnant or if she intends to become pregnant soon?

Although Title VII does not prohibit employers from asking applicants or employees about gender-related characteristics such as pregnancy, such questions are generally discouraged. The EEOC will consider the fact that an employer has asked such a question when evaluating a charge alleging pregnancy discrimination. Adverse decisions relating to hiring, assignments, or promotion, that are based on an employer's assumptions or stereotypes about pregnant workers' attendance, schedules, physical ability to work, or commitment to their jobs, are unlawful.

4. Is an employee or applicant protected from discrimination because of her past pregnancy?

Yes. An employee or applicant may not be subjected to discrimination because of a past pregnancy, childbirth, or related medical condition. For example, an employer would violate the PDA by terminating an employee shortly after she returns from medically-related pregnancy leave following the birth of her child if the employee's pregnancy is the reason for the termination. Close proximity between the employee's return to work and the employer's decision to terminate her, coupled with an explanation for the termination that is not believable (e.g., unsubstantiated performance problems by an employee who has always been a good performer), would constitute evidence of pregnancy discrimination.

5. What are examples of medical conditions related to pregnancy or childbirth?

Medical conditions related to pregnancy may include symptoms such as back pain; disorders such as preeclampsia (pregnancy-induced high blood pressure) and gestational diabetes; complications requiring bed rest; and the after-effects of a delivery. *(For information about the application of the ADA to pregnancy-related medical conditions, see Question 17.)*

Lactation is also a pregnancy-related medical condition. An employee who is lactating must be able to address lactation-related needs to the same extent as she and her co-workers are able to address other similarly limiting medical conditions. For example, if an employer allows employees to change their schedules or use sick leave for routine doctor appointments and to address non-incapacitating medical conditions, then it must allow female employees to change their schedules or use sick leave for lactation-related needs.

In addition to being protected under the PDA, female hourly employees who are breastfeeding have rights under other laws, including a provision of the Patient Protection and Affordable Care Act that amended the Fair Labor Standards Act to require employers to provide reasonable break time and a private place for breast-feeding employees to express milk. The Department of Labor has published a Fact Sheet providing general information on the break time requirement for nursing mothers: **www.dol.gov/whd/regs/compliance/whdfs73.htm**.

6. Does the law provide protections for caregivers?

Discrimination based on an employee's caregiving responsibilities may violate Title VII if it is based on sex. For instance, an employer would violate Title VII by denying job opportunities to women, but not to men, with young children, or by reassigning a woman who has recently returned from maternity leave to less desirable work based on the assumption that, as a new mother, she will be less committed to her job. Although leave related to pregnancy, childbirth or related medical conditions can be limited to women affected by those conditions, if an employer provides parental leave, it must be provided to similarly situated men and women on the same terms. In addition, employers covered by the FMLA must provide eligible employees with up to 12 weeks of job-protected leave to care for and bond with a newborn baby or a recently adopted child. Discrimination based on an employee's caregiving responsibilities may violate the ADA if it is based on the employee's relationship with an individual with a disability. *(See Question 21.)*

7. Will an employer violate the PDA if it takes an adverse action against a pregnant worker based on concerns about her health and safety?

Yes. Although an employer may, of course, require that a pregnant worker be able to perform the duties of her job, adverse employment actions, including those related to hiring, assignments or promotion, that are based on an employer's assumptions or stereotypes about pregnant workers' attendance, schedules, physical ability to work or commitment to their jobs, are unlawful. Even when an employer believes it is acting in an employee's best interest, adverse actions based on assumptions or stereotypes are prohibited. For instance, it is unlawful for an employer to involuntarily reassign a pregnant employee to a lower paying job involving fewer deadlines based on an assumption that the stress and fast-paced work required in her current job would increase risks associated with her pregnancy.

An employer may only reassign a pregnant worker based on concerns about her health or the health of her fetus if it can establish that non-pregnancy or non-fertility is a BFOQ as described in Question 2. In very few, if any, situations will an employer be able to establish this defense.

8. May an employer take an adverse action against a pregnant worker because of the views or opinions of co-workers or customers?

No. Just as an employer cannot refuse to hire or retain a pregnant woman because of its own prejudices against pregnant women, it cannot take an adverse action against a pregnant worker because of the prejudices of co-workers, clients, or customers. For instance, an employer may not place a pregnant worker who can perform her job on leave based on her co-workers' belief that she will place additional burdens on them and interfere with their productivity.

9. Does the PDA protect employees from harassment based on pregnancy, childbirth or related medical conditions?

Yes. Unwelcome and offensive jokes or name-calling, physical assaults or threats, intimidation, ridicule, insults, offensive objects or pictures, and interference with work performance that is motivated by pregnancy, childbirth or related medical conditions may constitute unlawful harassment. Whether the conduct is sufficiently hostile to constitute unlawful harassment depends on factors such as the frequency of the conduct or its severity. Employer liability can result from the conduct of supervisors, co-workers or non-employees such as customers or business partners over whom the employer has some control.

10. May an employer exclude pregnant workers from access to light duty (temporary work that is less physically demanding than an employee's normal duties)?

An employer may not deny an employee light duty because she is pregnant. Some employer light-duty policies may not explicitly exclude pregnant employees, such as policies of providing light duty only to employees who are injured on the job and/or who have disabilities within the meaning of the ADA, but may still violate the PDA if they impose significant burdens on pregnant employees that cannot be supported by a sufficiently strong justification. For example, one way a pregnant employee could demonstrate a significant burden is to show that her employer accommodates a large percentage of nonpregnant employees with limitations under its policy while denying accommodations to a large percentage of pregnant employees. If the employer did not have a sufficiently strong justification for such a policy, an inference of discrimination would arise.

11. May an employer require a pregnant employee who is able to perform her job to take leave at any point in her pregnancy or after childbirth?

No. An employer may not force an employee to take leave because she is or has been pregnant, as long as she is able to perform her job. Requiring leave violates the

PDA even if the employer believes it is acting in the employee's best interest. If an employee has been absent from work as a result of a pregnancy-related condition and then recovers, her employer may not require her to remain on leave until the baby's birth; nor may an employer prohibit an employee from returning to work for a certain length of time after childbirth.

12. May an employer impose greater restrictions on pregnancy-related medical leave than on other medical leave?

No. Under the PDA, an employer must allow women with physical limitations resulting from pregnancy to take leave on the same terms and conditions as others who are similar in their ability or inability to work. Thus, an employer:

- may not fire a pregnant employee for being absent if her absence is covered by the employer's sick leave policy;

- may not require employees limited by pregnancy or related medical conditions to first exhaust their sick leave before using other types of accrued leave if it does not impose the same requirements on employees who seek leave for other medical conditions;

- may not impose a shorter maximum period for pregnancy-related leave than for other types of medical or short-term disability leave; and

- must allow an employee who is temporarily disabled due to pregnancy to take leave without pay to the same extent that other employees who are similar in their ability or inability to work are allowed to do so.

An employer must also hold open a job for a pregnancy-related absence for the same length of time that jobs are held open for employees on sick or temporary disability leave. If the pregnant employee used leave under the FMLA, the employer must restore the employee to her original job or to an equivalent job with equivalent pay, benefits and other terms and conditions of employment.

Note that under the ADA, an employer may have to provide leave in addition to that provided under its normal leave policy as a reasonable accommodation for someone with a pregnancy-related impairment that is a disability. *(For more information about making reasonable accommodations under the ADA, see Questions 22-24.)*

13. Must an employer provide leave to bond with, or care for, a newborn (called "parental leave" in the Guidance)?

Under the PDA, leave related to pregnancy, childbirth or related medical conditions may be limited to women affected by those conditions, but parental leave must be provided to similarly situated men and women on the same terms. If, for example, an employer extends leave to new mothers beyond the period of recuperation from childbirth, it cannot lawfully refuse to provide an equivalent amount of leave to new fathers for the same purpose. In addition, the FMLA requires covered employers to provide 12 weeks of job-protected leave for covered employees to care for and bond with a newborn baby or a recently adopted child.

14. Are employers who provide health insurance benefits required to provide insurance that includes coverage of pregnancy, childbirth or related medical conditions?

Yes. Employers who have health insurance benefit plans must apply the same terms and conditions for pregnancy-related costs as for medical costs unrelated to pregnancy. If the plan covers pre-existing conditions—as all health plans are required to do as of January 1, 2014, under the Patient Protection and Affordable Care Act—then it must cover the costs of an insured employee's pre-existing pregnancy. If the plan covers a particular percentage of the medical costs incurred for nonpregnancy-related conditions, it must cover the same percentage for pregnancy-related expenses.

Employers can violate the PDA by providing health insurance that excludes coverage of prescription contraceptives, whether the contraceptives are prescribed for birth control or for medical purposes. To comply with Title VII, an employer's health insurance plan must cover prescription contraceptives on the same basis as prescription drugs, devices and services that are used to prevent the occurrence of medical conditions other than pregnancy. For example, if an employer's health insurance plan covers preventive care for medical conditions other than pregnancy, such as vaccinations, physical examinations or prescription drugs to prevent high blood pressure or to lower cholesterol levels, then prescription contraceptives also must be covered.

15. May employers covered by the PDA refuse to provide coverage of prescription contraceptives if they have religious objections to doing so?

In *Burwell v. Hobby Lobby Stores, Inc.*, 134 S. Ct. 2751 (2014), the Supreme Court ruled that the Patient Protection and Affordable Care Act's contraceptive mandate violated the Religious Freedom Restoration Act (RFRA) as applied to closely held for-profit corporations whose owners had religious objections to providing certain types of contraceptives. The EEOC's Enforcement Guidance explains Title VII's prohibition of pregnancy discrimination; it does not address whether certain employers might be exempt from Title VII's requirements under the RFRA or under the First Amendment.

16. How can a pregnant worker prove that an adverse action was the result of pregnancy discrimination under the PDA?

A PDA violation will be found if an employee's pregnancy, childbirth or related medical condition was a motivating factor in an adverse employment action. Evidence of discriminatory motive may include an explicit policy that treats pregnant workers less favorably; statements of decision-makers demonstrating pregnancy bias; close timing between an adverse action and a decision-maker's knowledge of the employee's pregnancy, childbirth or related medical condition; and more favorable treatment of employees of either sex who are not affected by pregnancy but who are similar in their ability or inability to work.

Discrimination may also occur when a neutral policy or practice has a disparate (or disproportionate) impact on pregnant employees if an employer cannot show that the policy or practice is job-related and consistent with business necessity. Examples may include policies that exclude pregnant employees from access to light duty or leave.

17. Must new mothers be provided with time off and space to express milk?

One of the first provisions of the Affordable Care Act (AKA Obamacare) to go into effect was a provision requiring most employers to provide hourly employees who want to express milk with necessary break times to do so and a private space that is not a bathroom to do so. Employers should make sure that new mothers know about this and should never punish an employee for taking such breaks.

8

How to Derail
Discrimination Charges

Oak Community Hospital prided itself on diversity. Older workers and minorities were actively recruited; women and men were given equal consideration for promotions, which were based solely on proven abilities and accomplishments.

So the general director was shocked to learn that the hospital was the target of an age discrimination suit, and the plaintiff was a woman who had been dismissed after only several months for making hundreds of dollars' worth of personal long-distance calls on a hospital phone.

Why should the hospital spend its limited funds on paying lawyers to handle the suit, which was tantamount to harassment? Still, the general director reflected, if the woman was irrational enough to bring the suit in the first place, maybe she really believed she might regain her old job by threatening a lawsuit.

The Long Arm of Title VII

The most far-reaching law pertaining to the day-to-day application of federal rules for the workplace is Title VII of the Civil Rights Act of 1964. It bars discrimination based on race, sex, color, religion and national origin. Over the years, this law has been extensively amended by Congress and interpreted by the courts to apply to a wide variety of situations.

Basically, the act makes it unlawful for an employer "to fail or refuse to hire or to discharge or otherwise discriminate against any individual with respect to his compensation, terms, conditions or privileges of employment because of such individual's race, color, religion, sex or national origin."

Title VII covers all employers with 15 or more employees for each working day in 20 or more calendar weeks in the year. The EEOC, which administers the law, handles an average of 75,000 to 80,000 complaints annually.

Initially, Congress passed the law as a ban on discrimination in hiring blacks. But its scope has been expanded to cover firings and layoffs, affirmative action, reverse discrimination and opportunities for advancement, as well as sexual harassment. (A separate law, the Equal Pay Act of 1963, specifically protects women's pay levels. The EEOC also administers that law.)

Many employers are well versed in Title VII and avoid the obvious pitfalls, such as advertising for "white males." Companies are aware that recruitment must be "color blind" to ensure a diverse labor force. Screening procedures can't block out a race or gender by being too demanding, such as requiring a college degree for secretarial work. Still, you can be selective in your job screening if you can demonstrate "business necessity." That's not easy to do because race, color, religion, sex or national origin can in no way appear to be a factor in a hiring decision.

You can demonstrate business necessity by showing the following:

- Selectivity is required for the safe and efficient operation of the business.

- It effectively carries out the purpose that it's supposed to serve.

- No alternative policies or practices would better or equally serve the same purpose with less discriminatory impact.

There's also a single, narrow exception to the ban against a hiring decision based on race, color, religion, sex or national origin: If you can show a bona fide occupational qualification where the position requires specific standards, you can select your job candidate regardless of race, creed and so forth.

The Equal Employment Opportunity Commission has issued guidance stating that Title VII prohibition of discrimination based on sex covers discrimination against sexual orientation or gender identity as well. The EEOC has intervened in several cases where employers have discriminated against employees who have begun sex reassignment procedures. In addition, in early 2016, the agency filed two federal lawsuits—one in Maryland and one in Pennsylvania—in which it is alleging for the first time that Title VII's sex discrimination prohibition includes prohibiting discrimination based on all forms of sexuality including sexual orientation and gender identity.

SEX DISCRIMINATION

Title VII and the Equal Pay Act require employers to ignore gender when making hiring and firing decisions.

In the past, employers tended to limit women to jobs not requiring extensive physical activity—a practice that's no longer tolerated. Nor is it lawful for employers to discriminate against women in the belief that their turnover rate is higher, they tend to take more sick leave or they may become pregnant. Also, during preemployment interviews, employers may not ask women applicants about any family plans or child care issues.

The new sex discrimination battleground appears to be discrimination against the lesbian, gay, bisexual and transgender communities. Two states, North Carolina and Mississippi, passed laws requiring individuals to use the public restroom corresponding to their birth sex regardless of how they identify. Both laws clash with the EEOC's position on bathroom usage by the transsexual.

EQUAL PAY ACT

The Equal Pay Act (EPA) prohibits employers from paying one gender less than the other if they have jobs that require equal skill, effort and responsibility and if those jobs are performed under similar conditions.

The biggest impact of this law was to end dual pay scales for men and women. The only exceptions to the equal pay regulations are:

• A seniority system or a merit system.

• A system that measures earnings by quantity or quality of production.

• A differential based on factors other than gender, such as educational level and years of experience.

Interpreting the EPA, courts have held that the jobs need not be identical, only "substantially equal." As spelled out in one ruling, "insubstantial differences in the skills, effort and responsibility requirements should be ignored."

Also, in 2009, Congress passed the **Lilly Ledbetter Fair Pay Act**, which makes it easier for women and others to sue for pay discrimination that may date back decades. Retroactive to May 2007, the law liberalizes statutes of limitations on when employees can file such lawsuits.

Drafted in response to the 2007 U.S. Supreme Court decision in *Ledbetter v. Goodyear Tire & Rubber*, which said employees had at most 300 days to file pay discrimination complaints, the new law counts each unfairly low paycheck as a fresh discriminatory act. It caps damages at $300,000 and retains current limits on back pay to two years' worth.

The Ledbetter Fair Pay Act amends Title VII to make clear that each allegedly unfair paycheck shall be considered a fresh incident of discrimination.

SEXUAL HARASSMENT

The courts are actively advancing the concept of sexual harassment under guidelines spelled out by the EEOC: "Unwelcome sexual advances, requests for sexual favors, and other verbal or physical conduct of a sexual nature constitute sexual harassment when (1) submission to such conduct is made either explicitly or implicitly a term or condition of an individual's employment; (2) submission to or rejection of such conduct by an individual is used as the basis for an employment decision affecting such individual; and (3) such conduct has the purpose or effect of substantially interfering with an individual's performance or creating an intimidating, hostile or offensive work environment."

In two landmark cases in 1998, the U.S. Supreme Court adopted a strict standard holding employers liable for supervisors who sexually harass their employees. "An employer is subject to vicarious liability to a victimized employee for an actionable hostile environment created by a supervisor with immediate (or successively higher) authority over the employee," the court held in *Burlington Industries, Inc. v. Ellerth*, 524 U.S. 742 (1998) and *Faragher v. City of Boca Raton*, 524 U.S. 775 (1998).

Moreover, the court ruled, the employee claiming the discrimination doesn't even have to prove that she suffered any "adverse employment action." That means the "victim" doesn't have to prove, for example, that she was discriminated against in a promotion or that she was demoted or fired—yet the employer is still presumed liable by the courts.

One bit of good news in the court's decisions: You can escape liability for the harassment caused by your supervisors, but you have to jump over some tough hurdles to do so. Here's what you need to prove:

- You took no tangible adverse employment action against the victim.

- You exercised reasonable care to prevent and *promptly* correct any sexually harassing behavior.

- The employee unreasonably failed to take advantage of any preventive opportunities provided by your company, or she failed to avoid harm otherwise.

In 2004, the Supreme Court carved out an exception to this rule. If the harassment is so egregious that it forces the victim to quit her job, it doesn't matter what rules the employer had in place for handling complaints. The employer can be held liable even if the worker never uses the internal complaint procedures. (*Pennsylvania State Police v. Suders*, 124 S. Ct. 2342)

In another Supreme Court decision in 1998 the court held that same-sex harassment can be actionable under Title VII. (*Oncale v. Sundowner Offshore Services, Inc.*, 523 U.S. 75, 1998) The court's decision in *Oncale* resolved the conflict between a number of federal appeals courts over whether individuals could bring claims of sexual harassment when the alleged harasser was the same sex as the victim.

In *Oncale* the justices stressed that neither of the parties has to be homosexual in order for same-sex harassment to occur. Rather, the harassment must be "because of sex." It is important to note that the court reiterated that Title VII does not require "asexuality nor androgyny" in the workplace; it forbids only behavior that is so objectively unreasonable that it alters the "conditions" of the victim's employment. Based on the *Oncale* case, you should investigate claims of same-sex harassment as vigorously as you do claims of harassment between genders.

Moreover, realize that bullying behavior that's directed at one sex but not another can also be sexual harassment, such as screaming at only female employees. (*EEOC v. NEA*, 9th Cir., 2005)

Preventing harassment

As the EEOC recognizes in its enforcement guidance on sexual harassment, prevention is the best means to reduce the occurrence and impact of sexual harassment in the workplace. The EEOC encourages employers to:

> *Take all steps necessary to prevent sexual harassment from occurring, such as affirmatively raising the subject, expressing strong disapproval, developing appropriate sanctions, informing employees of their right to raise, and how to raise, the issue of harassment under Title VII, and developing methods to sensitize all concerned.*

In general, an employer can minimize its exposure to workplace harassment by (1) implementing an accessible, strongly articulated and meaningfully enforced sexual harassment policy and (2) acting promptly and effectively to remedy complaints.

Develop a Clear, Written Policy

You should develop a written policy containing these elements:

- A broad definition of the types of conduct that constitute sexual harassment.
- A statement that offenders will be subject to appropriate discipline.
- A statement encouraging employees who feel victimized to report the conduct.
- A statement requiring employees and supervisors to report any offensive conduct they experience or witness.
- A statement providing assurances that no employee will be retaliated against for reporting the harassment.
- A statement indicating that all reports of sexual harassment will be promptly and thoroughly investigated, and that prompt remedial action will be taken should the company conclude that sexual harassment has occurred.

Develop a Complaint Procedure

You should develop a procedure for reporting and resolving sexual harassment complaints and indicate this in your written policy. The procedure should designate the person(s) or specific position(s) responsible for handling those complaints. This individual should be someone other than the employee's direct supervisor.

Ensure confidentiality to the extent practical. The National Labor Relations Board ruled that employers cannot force employees to keep what they know about investigations confidential. The NLRB ruled that such rules would discourage workers from discussing workplace conditions in violation of the National Labor Relations Act (NLRA). Inform employees of the NLRA's restrictions and also explain the company may have to disclose the origin or nature of the complaint to resolve it or impose the proper discipline.

Your complaint procedure should be communicated to employees, including supervisors, via the employee handbook or other documents. You should obtain and file written acknowledgments from all employees stating that they've received and read the policy. Also, post the policy in a conspicuous place.

Hold Training Sessions

In some cases employees may not realize that their conduct constitutes sexual harassment. You should provide periodic training sessions for employees on how to identify this type of behavior. Such training sessions are also an opportunity for you to further publicize your policy. Outline the type of conduct and speech that can constitute sexual harassment, and emphasize the possible economic consequences that can result for both the employer and the offending employee. Also, require employees to sign a statement indicating that they attended the training.

The most effective training is interactive and provides a different take on the issues. Avoid repeating the same training over and over again. Employees will simply tune out. In California, many employers are required to provide sexual harassment training. Consult with your attorney to ensure you are meeting your state's requirements.

Promptly Investigate and Take Corrective Action

Employees should be aware that you will promptly investigate allegations of sexual harassment and will take appropriate corrective action after completing your investigation. Your investigation should include interviewing the victim, the alleged harasser and witnesses. Then you should take corrective action to stop the offending conduct; this is key to your defense should the case end up in litigation.

Be proactive

Many irritations fester until they become complaints to outside agencies like the EEOC, when a little internal attention might have remedied the situation if only the employer had known about it. But the victims of harassment often don't know whom they can trust in management.

Many courts have found employers liable for harassment, especially by supervisors, because management sat on its hands when harassed individuals went to higher-ups with their complaints. Many employers have found a grievance setup particularly helpful in handling sexual discrimination and harassment complaints. If the process has several levels, all the better, if only to assure complainants that they'll get an objective hearing from someone far removed from the scene of the alleged "crime."

When your investigation reveals that a complainant has a legitimate grievance, you are expected to do *something*. In many cases a warning will be sufficient. But if the harasser's behavior doesn't stop or was truly outrageous, you may want to demote or fire him or her, especially if the culprit is a supervisor. Also, if a complainant has suffered from a job discrimination action, such as the loss of a promotion or a raise, correct the injustice as soon as possible.

If you receive a complaint and it's found to be legitimate, you should make a point of reiterating your policy against sexual harassment. This will help deter the individual who's been accused, reassure the complainant and serve as a message to other workers that you intend to play fair.

Guard against lawsuits by alleged harassers

In recent years, a growing number of employees who've been terminated or disciplined for engaging in sexual harassment have sued their employers. Their claims have included breach of contract, intentional infliction of emotional distress, interference with contractual relations, discrimination, defamation and federal conspiracy charges.

In addition, public employers must be concerned about constitutional claims or state statutory claims, such as those arising from protections afforded by civil service statutes. Unionized employers must be alert to claims that discipline was improperly imposed under the terms of a collective bargaining agreement.

Generally, a thorough investigation can minimize an employer's liability for claims made by an alleged harasser. As noted earlier, you must keep confidential any allegations of sexual harassment and all documents and conversations relating to the investigation. However, during an investigation the allegations or the complainant's identity may have to be disclosed to resolve the complaint, so employees should be made aware of this fact. Any statement about the alleged harassment should be as objective as possible and not accusatory in nature.

An employer has a qualified privilege to make a statement about the alleged harassment if it's done in good faith and for a proper purpose to someone who has a legitimate need to receive the information. But if the statement is made in a malicious or reckless manner, the employer may lose this qualified privilege and be subject to liability for defamation. The qualified privilege is also lost if there is excessive publication beyond the scope or need of the investigation.

To guard against discrimination claims, employers must also ensure that they are consistent in dispensing discipline and that the discipline doesn't have an unintended disproportionate impact on a protected class (by gender, race, religion, etc.).

NATIONAL ORIGIN AND RELIGION DISCRIMINATION

Title VII bars discrimination based on an employee's national origin. This includes channeling immigrants into specific types of positions. Some employers, who have only hired Hispanic applicants for certain jobs, have been sued by non-Hispanic applicants who felt they were denied consideration because they were born in America. Similarly, ethnic restaurants that only hire immigrants from the country of the food served have run into similar claims.

Religious dress has also been a controversial topic. Title VII requires employers to accommodate religious practices as long as doing so does not constitute an "undue burden" on the employer.

In *EEOC v. Abercrombie & Fitch* (No. 14-86, 2015), a Muslim woman was discharged for wearing a headscarf. She filed a religious discrimination charge against the employer, which countered that the woman had never requested a religious accommodation. The Supreme Court ruled she could proceed with her lawsuit anyway.

Employers must be flexible in enforcing dress codes and grant accommodations to employees for religious garb when doing so is not an undue burden. Further, when an employer knows the employee wears the clothing because of a deeply held belief, it must weigh possible accommodations even if the employee does not specifically request a religious accommodation under Title VII of the Civil Rights Act.

COURT LOWERS THE BAR ON JOB-BIAS SUITS

Your company's chances of winning a job discrimination lawsuit grew slimmer after a U.S. Supreme Court ruling in an ADEA case. The court ruled unanimously that plaintiffs don't need direct evidence that their employer intended to discriminate against them. Workers have to show only that they suffered adverse treatment (like firing or demotion) and that the company's explanation for it was false. Then a jury could decide whether the company's real motive was discriminatory. (*Reeves v. Sanderson Plumbing Products*, 530 U.S. 133)

In a sex discrimination case, the High Court ruled that direct evidence of discrimination was not necessary for the employee to prevail. (*Desert Palace v. Costa*, 123 S. Ct. 2148)

AGE DISCRIMINATION

The Age Discrimination in Employment Act (ADEA) protects individuals who are 40 years of age and older. It applies to employers that have 20 or more workers for each working day in 20 or more calendar weeks in the current or preceding year. The ADEA bars employers from refusing to hire a job candidate based on age alone, and it protects employees from layoffs on the same basis.

Under the ADEA, once a claimant makes a *prima facie* case of age discrimination, the burden of proof shifts to the employer. To raise a *prima facie* case, in the absence of direct evidence, a plaintiff must show that he or she is within the protected age class, was qualified for the position at issue and was discriminated against despite being qualified.

Most age discrimination cases grow out of wrongful discharge and mandatory retirement policies, but they can involve any adverse change in working conditions, including denial of a promotion or training.

An employer may defend itself on several grounds:

- **The employee's age represented** a bona fide occupational qualification (BFOQ): that is, an older worker could not perform the job by virtue of his or her age. (For example, age qualifies as a BFOQ for pilots, who can't receive FAA certification if they are older than age 65.) Be very careful and consult legal counsel before relying on the BFOQ argument.

- **The employee was terminated** for just cause, which may be based on misconduct, unsatisfactory performance or incompetence.

- **The employee was discharged** for business necessity. In this defense the employer must prove the existence of valid business reasons, unrelated to age, that required the termination of the employee. These might include a major company reorganization because of financial difficulties.

An employer will often defend an ADEA case on the ground that the disputed employment decision was not based on age, but rather on "reasonable factors other than age. . . ." [29 U.S.C. §623(f)(1)] Although "other reasonable factors" is written into the statute as a defense, it is usually not pleaded as an affirmative defense. In general, the higher cost of salary, overqualification and lesser years of remaining service are not considered "reasonable factors other than age" because they are so closely related to age. These reasons are frequently called "proxies" for age, and a defense based on one of these grounds probably won't be successful.

A 1986 amendment to the ADEA bans mandatory retirement at any age (except for certain firefighters and law enforcement officers), regardless of early retirement provisions in an employee benefits plan or seniority system. Employees may still elect early retirement at a specified age or at their option. (Check your state and local laws for additional restrictions, which might disallow mandatory retirement ages or other involuntary termination of older workers.)

➤ **Observation:** The prohibition against mandatory retirement doesn't apply to employees who are at least 65 and who, for the two years immediately preceding retirement, are employed in a high policy-making or bona fide executive position and are entitled to receive employer-financed pensions or other retirements benefits of at least $44,000 annually.

Note that in 1996 the U.S. Supreme Court said employees alleging that their employer violated the ADEA don't have to show that they were replaced by someone under the age of 40. Rather, they simply have to show that they are 40 or more years of age and substantially older than their replacement. The court stated that "the fact that a replacement is substantially younger than the plaintiff is a far more reliable indicator of age discrimination than is the fact that the plaintiff was replaced by someone outside of the protected class." The plaintiff in the case was a 56-year-old regional manager who was discharged after his employer reorganized its geographic sales territories. His territory was taken into another, and a 40-year-old was named manager of the new region. Unfortunately, it's not clear what is meant by "substantially younger." (*O'Connor v. Consolidated Coin Caterers Corp.*, 519 U.S. 1040, 1996)

Waivers under the OWBPA

If you have to terminate workers, it's a smart move to ask them to sign an agreement waiving their right to sue for discrimination or wrongful discharge. But that's not enough if the worker is over 40 years old because he or she could also sue you for age discrimination under the ADEA.

To protect yourself, you must put an additional provision in your waiver agreement that specifically deals with ADEA claims. What's more, it will not be legally

---

WATCH OUT FOR YOUTH-BIAS CLAIMS

Under federal law, employees must be 40 or older to file an age-bias lawsuit. But several states—among them Maine, Michigan, New Jersey, New York and Oregon—don't have a minimum age at which legal protection begins. They either set no minimum or define "age" as older than 18 and have allowed youth-based discrimination claims.

Two cases in point:

- Kimberly Zanni, a 31-year-old account executive, was fired and replaced by an older, less qualified woman. One supervisor had told Zanni that she sounded too young on the phone and that her clients wanted an older account exec. Zanni sued for age discrimination under Michigan's Civil Rights Act, and the state court of appeals let the case go to trial. The court said the state law, which forbids bias on the basis of "chronological age," also covers employees under 40. (*Zanni v. Medaphis Physician Services Corp.*, 463 Mich. 878, 618 N.W. 2d 596)

- In 1999 the New Jersey Supreme Court ruled that its state law protected a 25-year-old bank vice president who was fired after the bank's chairman discovered his age. (*Bergen Commercial Bank v. Sisler*, 157 N.J. 188, 723 A. 2d 944)

Caution: This trend is still in its infancy, but it will catch on.

binding unless you also give the worker some extra benefit in return, such as extra severance pay or additional health care coverage.

But you're still not done yet. To be valid, ADEA waiver agreements must comply with all the requirements spelled out in a 1990 amendment to the ADEA, the Older Workers Benefit Protection Act (OWBPA). The amendment states that ADEA waivers are legal only when workers sign them in a "knowing and voluntary" manner. A waiver applying to an individual worker will meet OWBPA's requirements as long as it:

- Is written so that the employee can clearly understand it and refers specifically to age-discrimination rights and claims.

- Does not ask the worker to waive rights or claims that might come up after the waiver is executed.

- Offers the worker money or something else of value to which he or she otherwise would not be entitled.

- Advises the worker—in writing—to consult an attorney before signing it.

- Allows the worker at least 21 days to consider signing the agreement.

- Gives the worker at least seven days to revoke the agreement after signing it.

You face additional waiver hurdles whenever you fire, lay off or offer early retirement or severance packages to more than one employee. In these group situations, your waiver also must:

- Give workers at least 45 days, instead of 21, to consider the waiver agreement.

- Provide the job titles and ages of all individuals being laid off or being offered the same early retirement plan.

Caution: Make sure your age-bias waiver procedure is airtight. Workers still retain the right to sue if your waiver policy strays at all from the OWBPA, according to the Supreme Court's ruling in *Oubre v. Entergy Operations*, 522 U.S. 422 (1998).

The EEOC is vigorously prosecuting employers that violate the OWBPA. In particular, it has filed suit against several companies whose agreements state that the departing employee "hasn't filed and does not intend to file a discrimination charge." That's a violation of the law, the EEOC says. And employees who've refused to sign and then been laid off are joining the suits. Remember: Waivers must be voluntary. Signs of coercion will bring the wrath of the EEOC.

➤ **Recommendation:** Run a statistical check on retirement plans before putting them into effect to ensure they don't have an adverse impact on older workers. Special rules apply to retirement plans that discriminate between groups of employees over age 40. When drafting retirement plans, consult an attorney.

YOUR ULTIMATE RIGHT STILL SURVIVES

With all the anti-discrimination rules in effect, how to deal with the regulations remains in your hands. Adhering to the ground rules avoids conflict and can be beneficial to your business.

There are prohibitions, of course, against firing for discriminatory reasons: age, sex, race or disability. Here, too, you've got protections as an employer, but you must know where you're potentially vulnerable.

Obviously, your intent is to avoid getting sued. Your EEO policy most likely spells out that discharge criteria apply to all employees, regardless of race, creed or color. But as well intentioned as this policy is, it is often not enough to avoid a discrimination suit. Title VII, for instance, not only bars discrimination based on race, religion, color, national origin and sex but also contains an anti-retaliation provision that prohibits discrimination against any employee because he or she opposed an unlawful employment practice, filed a charge or testified, assisted or participated in any manner in an investigation, proceeding or hearing under Title VII.

As all-encompassing as the anti-discrimination provisions are, you can still discharge workers safely under Title VII if you fire for justifiable, documented reasons:

■ **Unsatisfactory work.** If a worker performs inadequately, you have every right to let that individual go, regardless of race, sex, age, color or national origin as long as you hold all workers to the same standards and rules.

■ **Failure to adhere to company rules,** such as those dealing with tardiness, absence, vacations and drugs. Employees protected by Title VII are not given special privilege to violate company policy.

■ **Unsatisfactory behavior.** It's important for you to take a firm and fair stand, as much for your company's own reputation as for other employees to know that you are committed to a just personnel policy.

■ **Business necessity.** If you can show that you acted in the interest of the company in operating a safe and efficient business and that the discharge was not solely for the convenience of the business, you have a viable argument against a claim.

HOW TO AVOID GETTING SUED

Here are some rules of thumb to follow in avoiding discrimination charges:

✓ **Establish, in writing,** a firm no-discrimination policy, backed by training for all employees, managers and supervisors.

✓ **Make sure that your performance standards** are objective and are interpreted that way by managers.

✓ **Apply your standards evenhandedly** so that minorities, women and older workers are not singled out for punishment of infractions.

✓ **Make sure your workplace is harassment-free** and not a hostile environment for any group.

✓ **Document all disciplinary action taken,** including warnings and suspensions.

✓ **Put all your rules in writing.** That way, they are difficult to ignore, and your employees are made fully aware that yours is a nondiscriminatory company.

9

How to Stop Employee Crime Dead in Its Tracks

*I*t was simply too much to believe. On the first day the head of information services had called in sick in more than a year, company president Elaine Mills needed to look for some documentation for a bill he had submitted. Figuring that he wouldn't mind (he had been a good colleague for nearly five years), she opened his file drawer and pulled out the file marked "Bills Paid." As she looked for the item in question, she noticed that something didn't add up.

There were invoices marked "Paid" for computers, trips, car services and dozens of other items Elaine had never heard of. All of them had been signed by the head of accounting, another trusted employee.

A sickening feeling overcame her. More focused questions soon raced through her mind. How far had the corruption spread through the firm? Should she call the police or a private detective? How should she proceed?

Don't Be Naive

Whether you want to admit it or not, thieves, including your own employees, may be bleeding your company dry. Employee theft alone costs companies $44 billion annually, according to the U.S. Chamber of Commerce. In fact, 30% of all business failures are due to employee theft.

Even more incredible, the CEOs of many companies refuse to believe that they could have a serious security problem. Sometimes that belief may be justified, but in most cases, according to the experts, it's naive and untrue. One security expert with 40 years' experience in the field says that when consulting teams visit new corporate clients, they know they have a better than 50% chance of uncovering a major case of theft or financial manipulation and a 75% chance of finding a costly malpractice.

Although it may be impossible to achieve total security of company property with any system, certain steps can reduce the degree of loss an organization may be experiencing. It's important for your organization to conduct a loss-prevention review, adopt a clearly defined no-theft policy and know what disciplinary steps to take if you suspect an employee of stealing.

First, take these steps to beef up your security:

- Conduct a current inventory of your company's loss exposure.

- Review hiring practices to see if your pre-employment screening needs revision.

- Check on the honesty climate in your company.

- Establish internal controls in operations where exposures to theft are greatest.

- Consider buying access-control and intrusion alarm systems.

- Protect employees from identity theft.

INVENTORY YOUR VULNERABILITIES

A loss-prevention review and analysis should begin with a physical investigation of the premises. The person in charge should be looking for two things:

- **Physical features of layout, buildings** and outside surroundings that would invite unauthorized access.

- **Assets, by category, that would be worth stealing.** You should obtain a detailed list of all exposures to loss by theft, pilferage, etc., so that safeguards can be strengthened or added at the proper points.

To spot other indications of vulnerable areas, check company records of past incidents, reports submitted by your insurance company, employees' observations and supervisors' assessments of the adequacy of controls over valuable materials, supplies and records.

Thieves no longer have to enter your business physically to steal from you. The Internet offers clever thieves and hackers a portal to valuable digital information, including your bank account numbers, usernames and passwords. Have an Internet security specialist examine your information architecture to determine any vulnerabilities. Also, train your employees to avoid "phishing" expeditions where unsolicited emails ask for privileged information.

In a small business, the owner is, in effect, the security director: He or she can sense when something is not right just by walking around the plant or office, checking the records, observing employees and so forth. However, as the company grows, the security function should be centralized in a senior manager. This person should have the responsibility for working with key managers and consultants to ensure that proper security procedures are in place and are being followed.

An important internal safeguard is to review your hiring procedures and pre-employment screening. Publishers of the Reid Report studied 20,000 job applicants and concluded that 30% of the people wouldn't steal under any circumstances; 40% would take property, given the opportunity and little chance of being caught; and 30% were thieves at heart who would seek opportunities to steal. The obvious implication: You've won half the battle if you screen out the dishonest individuals at the prehiring stage.

However, background checking has been complicated in recent years by federal as well as state regulations. And, recently, the EEOC has pushed to "ban the box," meaning removal of any questions concerning past criminal convictions from job applications. The federal government has banned the box in federal hiring. Several states have enacted legislation to implement "ban the box"; employers in those states must not ask about criminal convictions until after they have made a conditional job offer to the applicant. Employers are asked to weigh any convictions in terms of their relevance to the job, the crime's severity and the time elapsed since the conviction. Nor can employers use evidence of the applicant's arrest as a factor if the applicant was not convicted of a crime.

Nevertheless, there are steps you can take:

■ **Get all the information.** Even if a conviction is revealed after you have extended a conditional job offer, you are free to ask for information concerning the event and verify it.

■ **Verify all the information.** To avoid any discrimination charges, you should verify all information, not just criminal convictions. Verifying academic and job experience will provide a more in-depth picture of the applicant.

■ **Query references in person or by telephone** rather than by a form letter. Ex-employers and associates are often afraid to put candid opinions in writing for fear that the record could serve as the basis for a lawsuit against them.

■ **When applicants are being considered for positions** where they'll handle cash, valuable property or information, don't skimp on the expense of conducting credit and character checks. It often pays to use an investigator who specializes in the type of person you're hiring—executive, technical engineer and so on—and let him do the pre-employment screening.

The Fair Credit Reporting Act (FCRA) requires you to notify and obtain written consent from an applicant before conducting a third-party credit or background check for hiring purposes. Make the release part of the employment application. Some states have passed laws limiting how employers could use adverse credit reports in hiring. Consult with your attorney to ensure you are complying with your state's laws. If you reject the applicant based on third-party information, you must disclose the information to him. *Note:* In 2004, Congress passed the Fair and Accurate Credit Transactions Act, which exempts employers from obtaining an employee's permission when investigating suspected misconduct in the workplace.

■ **Tell your hiring supervisors** what they may do and ask under federal and state civil rights laws. A rule of thumb: You can't ask any questions pertaining to age, race, religion, ethnic background, gender or disability.

■ **Check on temps, too.** Make sure the temp agency you use properly screens its applicants, and get those assurances in your contract.

Many employers have switched to written honesty tests for pre-employment screening since the passage of the Employee Polygraph Protection Act of 1988.

Caution: Be careful how you use written honesty tests. Many of the popular tests employers use have been challenged in court because they were originally psychological tests. Their use prior to making a conditional job offer violated the Americans With Disabilities Act.

Employers should verify the test's scientific validity before use, and tests should be considered as only one factor in the overall job-hiring process, which includes background credentials, prior job experience, skills, education, references and interviews. If you're interested in exploring whether pre-employment tests can help your organization, first make sure there's a business necessity for instituting such testing in your screening procedures.

IS HONESTY COMPANY POLICY?

Most data about why employees are honest in some organizations and not in others point to four basic factors: personal standards, job satisfaction, peer pressure and the likelihood of being discovered. These findings underscore the importance of ensuring that the ethical climate you've created does indeed carry through to all levels of supervision, down to the newest entry-level employee. Some critical questions to ask:

- *Do you have a clear-cut policy on what constitutes unacceptable behavior, which front-line supervisors convey to all employees?*

- *Are managers held accountable for observing the same standards as their people?*

- *Would you take prompt action in a case of serious dishonesty? Would you be willing to prosecute if necessary?*

- *Do your managers know how to fire people properly and legally?*

ESTABLISH ENFORCEABLE CONTROLS

A work area with poor housekeeping, sloppy records and lax control of stockrooms, inventory and accounting is an area just waiting to be ripped off. To let your people know you mean business when you talk loss prevention:
- Establish sound rules.
- Explain these rules to your employees and make sure they're followed.
- Use unannounced inspections, surprise audits and disciplinary measures if necessary.
- Have all transactions approved by two people and have an outside auditor review them annually.

Locks are the least expensive way to secure doors to buildings and storerooms, but they are by no means the only system to consider. Where security staffing is limited, more sophisticated devices can prove cost-effective in the long run. These include digital locks, magnetic card keys and "intelligent" locks. The latter can provide a complete record of who entered and left a room during a 24-hour period.

Radio transmitter tokens are the most ingenious of the new access-control systems, in which a tiny transmitter activates a door-unlocking mechanism. Transmitters can also be attached to mobile company property such as vehicles, laptop computers and cell phones. This allows the company to locate them at any time.

Potential property loss is an important factor in deciding whether to get an intrusion- detection alarm system. If you can lock up valuables in such a way that they'd be difficult to steal, you may be able to dispense with alarms altogether.

IF YOU SUSPECT AN EMPLOYEE OF STEALING . . .

Generally, you should handle allegations of employee theft the same way you investigate and discipline other types of misconduct. If you suspect an employee of illegally removing or appropriating company property, be sure to conduct a thorough investigation (interview witnesses, investigate the "scene of the crime," examine the "suspect" employee's personnel record) before you interview the employee. Be sure to document each and every step that you take.

When you're ready to talk to the employee about the alleged theft, be sure to follow your standard disciplinary guidelines. Many employee handbooks state in the disciplinary section that employee theft is serious misconduct, which can lead to immediate termination. If that is the case, by all means you have every right to dismiss the employee immediately once there's solid proof of the crime.

As with everything else in employment law, however, there are a few caveats:

■ **Along the broad spectrum of employee theft** there certainly are differences between stealing a ream of paper and taking home a computer. Depending on the work history between you and your employees, you may want to keep this in mind in judging the severity of the offense.

■ **You have every right to call in the local authorities** to report a case of employee theft. But be careful! You don't want to run to the police every time a box of pens disappears, and you don't want to call them in without relatively strong evidence.

■ **In cases of large-scale theft, however** (automobiles, computers, money, etc.), it probably would be wise to call in the local authorities to follow up on your preliminary investigation.

Tip: Employees engaged in embezzlement frequently are punctual, arrive early, leave late, don't take time off and have a perfect attendance record. That's how they hide their misdeeds for years. Consider a policy requiring at least some mandatory time off.

10

DEALING WITH WORKPLACE VIOLENCE

A lice was quietly working in her office when she heard someone yelling outside at the reception desk. As she got up to see about it, her secretary, Marsha, came running in. "He's back and he's got a gun!" It was Samuel, an ex-employee Alice had terminated for threatening other employees. He was in the lobby, demanding to see her.

Alice knew Samuel had taken his termination badly. Should she go out and try to talk to him? Should she call 911 first?

How should she protect Marsha and the 100 other employees, particularly the receptionist, who was face-to-face with Samuel?

WHAT'S YOUR RESPONSIBILITY?

Workplace homicide is the fourth leading cause of workplace fatalities. The problem is so acute that the FBI has issued a special report, "Workplace Violence Report," available at **www.fbi.gov**.

Although robbery-related incidents account for the highest percentage of on-the-job slayings, much workplace violence is employee on employee. The key triggers of violence: personality conflicts, work-related stress, family or marital problems including domestic violence, emotional or mental illness, firings, and drug and alcohol abuse.

Violence puts employers in a tricky situation. On the one hand, you can't control the behavior of your employees and clients—much less that of strangers who walk in off the street. But the courts say you do have a "duty of care"—a responsibility to keep your employees reasonably safe from both inside and outside forces. Employers may be held liable for their employees' actions conducted within the scope of their employment.

The key issues: whether violent attacks were foreseeable and whether the conduct occurred within the scope of employment.

As an employer, you can also be charged with negligent hiring of an individual who is prone to violence if you knew or should have known that hiring the person created an unreasonable risk of harm to others. The focus is on how adequately you performed a background check before hiring the person.

BEWARE OF VIOLATING THE ADA

The Americans with Disabilities Act prohibits employers from discriminating against a qualified person with a disability on the basis of the disability. Individuals are disqualified from jobs only if the disability's limitations create a significant risk or cannot be reasonably accommodated without undue hardship to the employer. If you're faced with terminating a violent employee, you must consider possible application of the ADA. However, there's a "direct threat" exception.

"Direct threat" means an individual poses a specific and significant risk of substantial harm to the health or safety of others—a risk that can't be eliminated by reasonable accommodation. In 2002, the U.S. Supreme Court ruled that employers may use the "direct threat" defense to refuse to hire someone or terminate an employee. (*Chevron v. Echazabal*, 536 U.S. 73)

In its enforcement guidance, the EEOC states that an employer never has to tolerate or excuse violence, threats of violence, stealing or the destruction of property. Thus an employee cannot escape discipline for violent behavior just because he or she claims that the violent behavior is due to a mental disability. Enforcing appropriate-behavior rules is always good company policy.

You can also be held responsible for "negligent supervision" or "negligent retention" of an employee. Negligent supervision arises when an employee injures a third party because the employer improperly trained or supervised him or her. Negligent retention involves instances in which a company keeps on the payroll an employee who it knows, or reasonably should know, poses a threat to others.

Be aware that you can be held liable for acts of workplace violence under OSHA's general duty clause or state workers' compensation statutes.

To avoid liability and protect your workers, you need to assess the risk of violence in your workplace and take appropriate steps to reduce those risks. A workplace violence prevention program should include a system for documenting incidents, procedures to follow when a violent incident occurs, and open communication between you and your workers.

OSHA offers advice on workplace violence prevention at **www.osha.gov.**

SCREEN APPLICANTS

Take these steps in the hiring process to screen out violent persons:

1. Use an employment application. Compare the application and the person's résumé to check for any inconsistencies.

2. Conduct a thorough background check, consistent with applicable law, on every applicant. Avoid inquiries that are broader than necessary to evaluate the applicant's fitness for the position. Obtain his or her consent before making any inquiries. Keep all personal information confidential.

3. Check if the applicant has ever been *convicted* of a felony. Note that some states restrict an employer's right to use criminal records in employment decisions *(see page 46).* In "Ban the Box" states, the employer must make a conditional job offer before inquiring about the applicant's criminal background. Generally, felony and misdemeanor convictions may be considered only to the extent to which they relate to the applicant's suitability for employment in the position. It's also important that you distinguish between arrests and convictions. Employment decisions based on arrest records violate both federal and state laws. The EEOC has taken the position that an employer cannot ask a potential employee about arrest records. Arrests do not prove guilt.

4. Conduct a thorough job interview. Don't hire an applicant who hasn't been interviewed. In addition to asking about convictions *(see above)*, you should ask about any gaps in the person's employment history.

Although you may be tempted to inquire about an applicant's physical or mental impairment that may cause violent behavior, you must avoid asking about the person's disability-related status. The ADA limits pre-employment inquiries regarding an applicant's disabilities.

5. Verify the information the applicant provides on his or her job application and in the interview.

6. Call all the references provided by the applicant. Many employers, wary of defamation lawsuits, won't supply much, if any, information to prospective employers in a reference check. Try to alleviate this problem by having the applicant sign authorization forms to release information.

DEALING WITH VIOLENT EMPLOYEES

You should have a clearly written policy stating that violence of any sort is prohibited (including physical assault, verbal assault and possession of weapons). State the consequences of violating the policy—discipline or termination—and post the policy in a prominent place.

Seven questions make up a "common law" of just cause for disciplining an employee:

1. Did the employer give the employee forewarning of the possible consequences of his or her conduct?

2. Was the employer's rule reasonably related to the orderly, efficient and safe operation of the business and to performance that the employer might reasonably expect of the employee?

3. Did the employer, before disciplining the employee, investigate whether the person had violated or disobeyed a rule?

4. Was the employer's investigation conducted fairly and objectively?

5. At the investigation did the individual "judging" the matter obtain substantial proof that the employee violated the workplace rule?

6. Has the employer applied its rules and penalties evenhandedly and in a non-discriminatory manner?

7. Was the discipline administered reasonably related to the seriousness of the violation and the employee's record?

SET UP AN ACTION PLAN

1. **Have a system of early detection,** and encourage employees to report any signs of trouble.

2. **Set up some form of nondisciplinary intervention.** Have a crisis-intervention team. Consult with medical and legal professionals as well as HR people. Use an Employee Assistance Program.

3. **Train all supervisors about security measures,** complaint procedures, ways to defuse the violence and/or remove the offending employee.

4. **Notify the police, if necessary.**

5. **Alert potential victims,** but keep in mind defamation and privacy concerns regarding the offending employee. Remove the offender as discreetly and securely as possible.

6. **Document every incident** and conduct a thorough investigation.

7. **Upgrade security systems.**

8. **Provide employees with guidelines** and procedures for emergency situations.

IF YOU FIRE THE PERSON . . .

Firings are one of the biggest catalysts for violence. To head off violence and liability, rethink the way you conduct a termination meeting. To avoid outbursts:

- **Keep the meeting private.** Have a witness, but don't invite others who have no reason to be present.

- **Cut the drama.** Never scream, "You're fired."

- **Let the employee vent.** Summarize the reasons in tangible, nonemotional terms. Then let the employee have his or her say without being interrupted.

- **Have the final paycheck ready.** This way, the person will take something positive away from the meeting and have no excuse to return.

Don't assume that terminating a potential troublemaker is legally sufficient. Although removing a menace from the workplace certainly makes sense, you can still face a lawsuit if that person returns to the office and harms someone.

"An employer's legal obligation doesn't necessarily end at the plant's gate," says Joseph Kinney, director of the National Safe Workplace Institute. "Someone may need counseling or a psychiatric evaluation. If you just fire someone and that's it, you can face legal liability if you didn't investigate the individual's condition or try to get that person some help."

For more information on workplace violence, visit **www.osha.gov**. You may also wish to view an online training video, *Violence on the Job*, which offers practical ways to identify violence-at-work risk factors, available at the National Institute for Occupational Safety and Health's website: **www.cdc.gov/niosh/docs/video/violence.html**.

_11_

DEALING WITH THE RIGHTS OF THE DISABLED

A ble Machine Industries started hiring disabled assemblers because it was the right thing to do. Only later did the company find out that it was also highly profitable. Assemblers with disabilities were reliable, motivated, efficient and had a far lower turnover rate than other worker groups. That was the company's experience in all cases but one: that of a young woman who was unreliable and unpleasant to her co-workers, disabled and nondisabled alike.

All attempts to deal equitably with her problems failed, and the company had documented a long series of oral and written warnings. Had the woman not been disabled, her termination would have been a foregone conclusion. But given her special situation, the company felt uncertain about whether to keep her or let her go.

THE AMERICANS WITH DISABILITIES ACT

The Americans with Disabilities Act, enacted in 1990, has become one of the thorniest issues in employment law today. Employers need to be careful at every stage of the employment process—from hiring to firing—and consult their legal counsel before making any ADA-related employment decision. All employers that have 15 or more employees must comply with the ADA.

This sweeping civil rights legislation for an estimated 43 million disabled people has made some revolutionary changes in almost every segment of American life: offices, schools, public transportation, phone service, restaurants, theaters, and multinational and small businesses alike. Passage of the ADA gave the disabled Title VII rights to combat employment discrimination and become full-fledged participants in the U.S. labor market.

In practice, however, the ADA proved much less potent a remedy for employment discrimination than Title VII, due in part to court decisions that chipped away at the definition of "disabled" until it no longer included people with conditions such as cerebral palsy, epilepsy, cancer and diabetes. As a result, plaintiffs lost 97% of ADA employment cases that went to trial in 2004.

In response, Congress passed the ADA Amendments Act of 2008 (the ADAAA), which took effect Jan. 1, 2009. The law expressly rejected several Supreme Court decisions and clarified and broadened the ADA's protections, bringing it closer in line with Title VII. The ADAAA offers disabled workers and employers much needed direction in an area of the law that has proved frustrating for both.

DEFINING 'DISABILITY'

The ADAAA dramatically expands the number of Americans who would be deemed "disabled" under the law, and thus entitled to job protections and "reasonable accommodations" for their disabilities. The law mandates these key changes:

■ **Redefines "major life activity."** The original ADA was vague about what constitutes a disability, casting it in terms of a condition that substantially limits a major life activity. The new law is specific about what those major life activities are. They "include, but are not limited to, caring for oneself, performing manual tasks, seeing, hearing, eating, sleeping, walking, standing, lifting, bending, speaking, breathing, learning, reading, concentrating, thinking, communicating and working." In addition, the law lists bodily functions that might limit on major life activities.

■ **Requires a broad reading of "disability."** Employers and courts are directed to be generous when determining whether someone is disabled. So, courts are now more likely to side with employees who sue for ADA violations.

■ **Takes "mitigating measures" out of the ADA picture.** Thus, devices used to decrease the severity of impairments (medication, hearing aids, wheelchairs, etc.) can't be considered when determining whether the person is a qualified "disabled" person. (Glasses or contact lenses don't count.)

➤ **Observation:** The ADAAA has resulted in a more than 38% increase in the number of disability discrimination complaints filed with the EEOC since it took effect in 2009. Employers who do not know the law will get snared in its ever-widening net.

WHO'S COVERED

The ADA protects qualified individuals with a disability as long as the individual can perform the job's essential functions with or without a reasonable accommodation. Some conditions, such as deafness, blindness or the inability to walk are obvious disabilities. Short-term conditions, generally those lasting less than six months, are not disabilities under the law.

Under the ADAAA, chronic conditions such as epilepsy, diabetes, HIV infection or severe forms of arthritis, hypertension or carpal tunnel syndrome are disabilities even if they are in remission or controlled by medication. Mental illnesses such as depression or bipolar disorder are disabilities, as is mental retardation.

Also under the ADA, employers can't take an adverse employment action against a nondisabled job applicant or employee who has an association with a disabled person; for example, a parent with a disabled child, the spouse of a disabled person or a person living with someone who has a disability. However, the ADA does not require you to provide reasonable accommodation for the person associated with a disabled individual, though you may have to provide time off under the FMLA.

The ADAAA protects individuals with a record of disability, such as a person whose cancer is in remission. Many employers can fall into the "regarded as" trap. This occurs when an employer regards a person as disabled when he or she is not.

The law doesn't regard sexual preference as being an impairment and specifically excludes homosexuality, bisexuality, transvestism and transsexualism. The ADA provides no protections for those suffering from pedophilia, exhibitionism, voyeurism and certain other sexual behavior disorders. Similarly, compulsive gamblers, kleptomaniacs and pyromaniacs also have no recourse under the ADA. Nor do those with psychoactive substance-use disorders resulting from current use of illegal drugs.

MAKING REASONABLE ACCOMMODATIONS

The ADA prohibits employment discrimination against "a qualified individual with a disability." That means "an individual with a disability who, with or without reasonable accommodation, can perform the essential functions of the employment position that such individual holds or desires."

You do, however, have some say in what are considered to be the "essential functions of the job." The ADA explains that "consideration shall be given to the employer's judgment as to what functions of a job are essential, and if an employer has prepared a written description before advertising or interviewing applicants for the job, this description shall be considered as evidence of the essential functions of the job."

Accommodation can be equated to modifications or adjustments in the workplace. Under the law, reasonable accommodations can include:

- Job restructuring.
- Part-time or modified work schedules.
- Reassignment to a vacant position.
- Acquisition or modification of equipment or devices.
- Appropriate modification of employment tests, training materials or policies; supplying qualified readers or interpreters.
- Leaves of absence.

The key to making reasonable accommodation is realizing what people's actual abilities and limitations are and matching them with the job's essential requirements.

THE DEFENSE OF UNDUE HARDSHIP

An employer's defense against providing reasonable accommodation is that it would cause an undue hardship. This determination will be made on a case-by-case basis and takes into consideration the size of the business (number of employees, type of facilities and budget), the type of operation and the cost of the accommodation.

Very few employers actually win this argument, but thorough preparation and documentation are key to persuading a judge or jury that an accommodation constitutes an undue hardship. First, an employer must detail all costs associated with the accommodation and show exactly how the accommodation would disrupt the worksite. Secondly, the employer must show that it lacks the resources to provide the accommodation and that no other reasonable accommodation is available.

You may also refuse to accommodate a disability if you can show the disabled person may pose a direct threat to the health and safety of others on the job or to himself or herself.

ESSENTIAL FUNCTIONS

Why is this so crucial? The law gives you the right to determine the essential functions of the job. But you must have a written job description to present as evidence. If you haven't evaluated your descriptions recently, or if you don't have any, you should first perform a job analysis to find out the essential functions of each position.

You should consider the following factors:

- Purpose—the reason for the job.

- Major tasks—those necessary to accomplish the purpose.

- Job setting—description of the workstation and conditions where the major tasks are performed.

- Worker qualifications—minimum requirements a worker must possess to perform the major tasks.

For each task, you must decide what physical or mental activity is needed to get the job done.

Caution: The law gives employers the right to determine the essential functions of the job and to present a written job description as evidence. But how well that job description stands up in court will depend on how closely it is tailored to the essential duties of the actual job. Simply formalizing discriminatory criteria by writing them into a job description certainly does not make such criteria legal. In fact, a written job description can also be used against you as evidence of discrimination.

WORKPLACE ACCOMMODATIONS

Making reasonable accommodations is not limited to changing the physical structure of the workplace. The law mentions job sharing, modified schedules, flextime, part-time work and other possibilities. So if a disabled person is qualified for the job, you may have to alter not only your workplace to accommodate the person but also the time frame in which the job is done.

You don't need to modify an employee's work schedule if such modification would significantly disrupt operations, posing an undue hardship. In that case, you must consider reassigning the person to a vacant position that would enable him or her to work the hours requested.

Reassignment is a reasonable accommodation of the last resort and is required if (1) there's no effective accommodation that will enable the person to perform the essential functions of the job or (2) all other reasonable accommodations would cause undue hardship. The employee may be reassigned only if he or she is qualified for the new position. The vacant position must be equivalent in terms of pay, status, benefits and geographical location. Employers are not required to create a new position as an accommodation, but may transfer the disabled worker to an existing vacant position.

Are you concerned you may overlook a possible accommodation? Check the Job Accommodation Network's interactive database at **www.askjan.org**. It walks employers and employees through possible accommodations based on the employee's medical restrictions. Document the process so that if the case goes to court, you can show you made a good faith effort to accommodate. JAN can also provide estimated costs of possible accommodations as well and may save the employer some money. JAN estimates that 58% of accommodations cost less than $500.

Increasingly, employees seek time off as a reasonable accommodation. EEOC enforcement guidance suggests that you may have to hold open an employee's job as a reasonable accommodation unless you can demonstrate that doing so would pose an undue hardship on your company. Federal courts, however, have uniformly held that an indefinite leave of absence is not a reasonable accommodation.

As far as the ADA's interaction with the Family and Medical Leave Act, the EEOC states that an employer should determine an employee's rights under each statute separately and then consider whether the ADA and FMLA overlap regarding the appropriate actions to take.

Caution: Remember that just because an employee has exhausted his or her FMLA leave doesn't necessarily mean that the person may not still be protected by the ADA.

PENALTIES FOR VIOLATIONS

All remedies for employment violations of the ADA are the same as those under Title VII. They are limited to reinstatement with back pay and other benefits, where applicable. The EEOC or its state agency counterpart handles all complaints.

You can win a case brought against you under the ADA by an employee if you did not actually know about the disability. In a recent case a federal appeals court held that, unlike race or sex discrimination cases, where there's seldom an issue of whether the employer knew that the worker was a member of a protected class, the ADA "does not require clairvoyance." The court said "simple logic" holds that if those who make a personnel decision do not know of a worker's disability, the decision cannot have been influenced by bias based on that disability.

To avail yourself of the "I-didn't-know" defense, your company must be able to show that it had no knowledge of an employee's medical condition. This means that good management practices are more important than ever. For example, before taking negative action against an employee, be diligent about checking his or her personnel files for any mention of a serious illness. Managers who miss such information in a personnel file and later claim they were unaware of an employee's condition will be on shaky ground in court.

If you find that an employee does have a medical condition, you can still take the personnel action, but you should make sure the disability isn't the underlying cause for that action. For example, if you know that the disability is forcing a worker to take more sick days than usual, you could land in trouble for firing that worker based on a poor attendance record.

Consider whether the employee could perform the essential functions of the job if given an accommodation that would not cause an undue hardship for the company. Case law exists showing that under certain circumstances an employer may have to give reasonable accommodation to an employee whose disability causes him or her to violate the employer's absentee policy. Needless to say, you should consult with your attorney to determine your obligations under the ADA and related laws.

12

WHEN YOU MUST GIVE ADVANCE NOTICE OF A JOB LOSS

*E*ven before she opened the envelope, Maria Corelli had a premo-
nition it was bad news. The biggest customer for the fine dining
room furniture produced by the company she had inherited from her
parents was dropping the line. The customer had decided to turn to
an overseas supplier.

*The news meant Maria would have to shut down operations at her company's
Michigan plant almost immediately. In fact, the wooden furniture end of the business had not been making money for some time; the bulk of the company's sales
and all its profits came from its cheap plastics line, produced at a high-tech factory
in California. But Maria had kept the Michigan plant in operation because it added
prestige to the brand name and because it was the business her parents had founded.
In fact, many of the craftspeople who worked there were the children of her parents'
workers.*

*But the market for their kind of furniture had diminished. Now, losing the Michi-
gan plant's biggest, most reliable customer meant the facility had to be shuttered and
the entire emphasis shifted to the California line. The sooner the decision was put into
effect, the better.*

THE WARN ACT

No longer can the boss summarily close down a major operation or lay off a significant chunk of the workforce—at least not without paying a heavy price.

The constraints on individual firings—that they cannot be for reasons of race, sex
bias or union activity, or because an employee has missed weeks of work with an
illness—don't come into play here. Quite simply, the reasons don't matter. If your
company is covered by the Worker Adjustment and Retraining Notification (WARN)
Act, you have to give 60 days' notice before a mass layoff or plant closing. Not doing
so can be even more expensive than keeping employees on the payroll.

Although the WARN Act has been in effect since 1989, it still catches managers by
surprise. No wonder. The kind of major business catastrophe that forces a plant shutdown or a large layoff has the brass running around trying to plug holes in a crum-
bling dam; there's no time to check out the technicalities of a statute they've never had
to cope with in the past.

Our advice? Learn about the WARN Act now, when no crisis is looming.

Who's Covered?

The WARN Act covers businesses that employ more than 100 workers (not counting employees who work an average of less than 20 hours a week). If you own a company with only four or five dozen employees, you needn't worry about the WARN Act. Although the statute says that Congress wants a business that is not covered nonetheless "to the extent possible, to provide notice to its employees about a proposal to close a plant or permanently reduce its workforce," that's just a wish, not a legal obligation: It can't be enforced in court.

The 100-employee trigger, however, is not as simple as it seems at first. What if you have 80 full-time employees and 30 other part-timers or workers who are on call when demand is high? You add up the number of hours that all your employees work, excluding overtime. If it totals more than 4,000 hours a week, your company is covered by the law. Be careful here. Don't assume you have to tally only the workers at the plant being closed. Coverage under the WARN Act is considered by the total number of employees who work for your organization. The only entities you don't have to consider are subsidiaries that can show they are operated independently.

One plus for management: When calculating employment, use the week that is 60 days before the shutdown or closing would take effect. If business has been deteriorating, you've probably been calling in part-timers less frequently, so there's a better chance then that you've escaped the act's reach. But don't try to get too fancy, such as by handing out a few pink slips early just to get below the 100-worker limit. DOL regulations say that if the week used for the employee count is not typical, another date or an average over a recent period may be used to activate WARN Act requirements.

Remember, too, that the operation may be in a state with a plant closing law that is more sweeping than the federal statute. Iowa employers with as few as 25 employees must provide early warning as must similar sized employee-owned firms in Michigan. The trigger is 50 employees in Hawaii, Maryland, New York, Tennessee and Wisconsin. Illinois and New Hampshire set the level at 75 employees on the payroll. The city of Philadelphia requires employers with 50 or more employees to provide notice.

60 Days' Notice Required

All employees affected by a plant closing or major layoff must receive notice in writing at least 60 days before they go off the payroll. (Employees entitled to receive notice under the law include hourly and salaried workers, as well as managerial and supervisory staff.) If all the workers are represented by a union, notifying the union is sufficient; otherwise, each worker must be told personally.

In addition, the state agency that oversees retraining of dislocated workers must be informed. So must the chief elected official of the local government, who may be the mayor of the town where the plant is located or, if it is outside an incorporated municipality, the county executive. If you haven't set a definite closing date, you can give a range of up to two weeks, but the notice has to be delivered 60 days before the first possible closing date.

You do have leeway in how to deliver the notice: in a pay packet, by hand or mail. But if you use the pay-packet method, the notice has to be different from the usual enclosures so that the worker will realize that it's special and important.

The notice has to be in employees' hands 60 days before the job ends. If it's mailed, it has to be sent early enough to be *delivered* 60 days before the layoff. But DOL regulations admit that, with the postal service being what it is, some notices may not be delivered on time even if you make a good-faith effort to give adequate notice. The regulations say that's OK as long as the mail date was early enough for most workers to have received it in time.

➤ **Recommendation:** Get a signed receipt for the notice. The regulations don't require it, but this extra effort can save a lot of grief later if workers deny that they knew of the planned layoffs. Also, don't make inaccurate statements in the notice. Avoid discussing the specific criteria used in deciding to implement the layoff, and emphasize that the downsizing was prompted by business circumstances. You don't want employees making discrimination claims against you based on the layoff notice.

WHEN IS NOTICE NECESSARY?

If the facility is being closed down, even temporarily, advance notice is required if 50 or more workers will lose their jobs during any 30-day period. That's 50 or more workers at a single site. What gets tricky is figuring out what constitutes a single site.

The key seems to be how you use your workers. If there's a plant on one side of town with 40 employees and a warehouse on the other side of town with 15 workers, the locations would be considered separate sites. Therefore, their closing would not require a WARN Act notice if the bosses, the workforces and the equipment they use are different. This is true even though the output of the factory is stored in and shipped from the warehouse. But if the two locations share a workforce and equipment—if fork lifts and operators are shifted from one site to the other as needed, for example—they will be counted as one site, and notice is required before closing the two locations.

Proximity isn't a central concern. Even two manufacturing operations next door to each other and owned by the same company will count as separate entities in figuring whether 50 persons are affected by a layoff if they are managed by different bosses and maintain totally separate workforces.

WARN Act notices are also required for large-scale layoffs, even if the plant continues operating. What is considered large scale? The WARN Act specifies two kinds of measurements:

- One involves straight calculations. If more than 500 workers lose their jobs, the obligation to give 60 days' notice is triggered.

- The other calculates whether the layoff involves one-third of the workers at the affected site, as long as that totals at least 50 employees.

In short, if 50 employees of a 250-person workforce are dismissed, no advance notice is necessary because that number is below the one-third figure. If 40 members of a 60-person workforce are being laid off, no advance notice is necessary because the total is below the 50-worker minimum. As long as fewer than 500 workers are being laid off, *both* the one-third and the 50-person indicators must be met before management must give advance notice.

If the layoff is expected to last less than six months, there's no need to give advance notice. You're also in the clear if a shorter layoff was expected, but after six months you are still not ready to bring back the workers. But notice must be given as soon as it becomes reasonably foreseeable that the layoff will exceed six months, and the DOL can challenge you on the issue of whether you should have foreseen the delay.

Take the example of a plant that shuts down for retooling. The job was expected to take five months but, in fact, took seven. The DOL says that if the employer "has experienced similar delays in previous retoolings, the employer may be liable under WARN for having failed to give notice." Protect yourself by having solid evidence of why you thought the layoff would be short, as well as documentation of what went wrong with the initial projections that made it infeasible to rehire the workers when expected.

➤ **Observation:** In tallying both the number of workers affected by a plant closing and the number in a mass layoff, the law looks at a 30-day period. But if the DOL thinks that a company is trying to evade the law by breaking a big layoff into two that are more than 30 days apart, it can aggregate separate layoffs over a 90-day period.

It still may pay, however, to lay off workers in waves, such as by closing down one department with 40 workers on May 1 and keeping another 30 workers on until Aug. 10. That way, you can avoid the law and put the first part of the scheme into effect immediately without the 60-day wait. If you let go 45 employees in the first wave and keep 15 on the payroll for the extra three months, you may end up ahead of the game and have an orderly shutdown that can maximize the salvage value of the assets at the plant.

Again, don't ignore state laws. In Maryland a workforce reduction of 25% and 15 or more employees activates the state statute; in Michigan it is 25 employees, regardless of what percentage of the workforce that number constitutes.

EXCEPTIONS: UNEXPECTED EVENTS

The 60 days' notice is not required if management simply could not have known 60 days ahead of time that it would have to close down an operation. But be careful: The government will take a much narrower view of what management should have been able to anticipate than most business executives would. In any case, you must give as much notice as is practicable, along with a brief statement of the reason for reducing the notice period.

The easiest case to make is a natural disaster. The government doesn't expect you to tell workers ahead of time about an earthquake, flood or hurricane that demolishes a plant or makes extensive, time-consuming repairs necessary. The issue gets sticky, though, if the unforeseen condition precipitating the layoff or closing is a business disaster. The situation must, according to the regulations, be "sudden, dramatic and unexpected."

What would fit that definition? Perhaps a strike at a component maker, a war overseas that makes a key raw material unavailable, a cancellation of standing orders from your largest customer or an order from pollution-control authorities to stop operating immediately. But the government will always probe for evidence that smart bosses would have planned for the event. Did your competitors expect that strike at the supplier and build up an inventory of the vital parts? Has the important customer been hinting for months that it might cancel? If so, the DOL will claim that the event should not have been unexpected.

A business can also get out of the obligation to give 60 days' notice of a shut-down but not of a mass layoff if it is teetering on the brink, and news of a planned shutdown would destroy the last remaining chance to snare the loan, investment or order that could pull the company through the crisis. But that exception, too, is going to be interpreted by the DOL to apply in only a few instances.

▶ **Recommendation:** When the going gets tough, most managers remain optimistic; the talent that makes it to the top slot isn't the sort that thinks that problems cannot be overcome. The energy goes into trying to work through today's issues and thinking about tomorrow's. But the WARN Act makes it vital to look ahead realistically. If odds are against the plant staying open, you can meet the law's obligation by giving a *conditional notice* of closing. It can't be a vague "We'll close unless things get better," but such a warning is allowed if tied to a specific event. You can tell affected workers, for example, "Unless the Acme contract is renewed when it expires in 30 days, your job will be eliminated in 60 days."

IF NOTICE ISN'T GIVEN . . .

It can be costly, but not disastrous. The first thing to know: Courts have no authority to enjoin a shutdown or layoff on the grounds that the WARN Act was violated; nor are punitive damages available in WARN cases.

Workers or their unions can demand the money they would have earned between the time they were let go and the 60-day anniversary of the day they got the news. That's not just salary or wages, but also all normal employee benefits. That means the company is stuck with reimbursement for medical expenses incurred during that time, which otherwise would have been covered by the company health insurance plan.

In fact, the cost is likely to be greater than normal payroll costs. For one thing, interest is likely to be added to the actual pay due. And if the workers go to court to get their money, you can be stuck with paying their legal fees. On top of that, at least one court decision has interpreted the 60 days' pay due as 60 times a normal daily rate—even though employees would have earned only about 45 days' pay (given a five-day workweek) had the notice been given two months before layoffs. You might also be subject to a civil penalty of up to $500 for each day of the violation.

Furthermore, although the law has a provision allowing a company to seek a lower penalty when it can demonstrate that it acted in good faith, the early rulings on the issue suggest that is not going to be a winner for management.

Any severance pay given the workers will be deducted from the amount due under the WARN Act as long as the company is not legally obligated to pay them the severance.

➤ **Recommendation:** If business troubles really pile up so fast that you must shut down in fewer than 60 days, consider keeping the workers on the payroll for a full 60 days anyway. It may save you money in the long run—they will start looking for other jobs and those who find them won't stay the full 60 days—and there may be tasks that workers can do to minimize the financial impact of the closing on the overall company. The goodwill engendered might also cut down on sabotage, which could result if workers are given only brief notice that they are losing their jobs.